DETECTING AND PREVENTING CLASSROOM CHEATING

EXPERTS IN ASSESSMENT™

SERIES EDITORS
THOMAS R. GUSKEY AND ROBERT J. MARZANO

Please call our toll-free number (800–818–7243)
or visit our website (www.corwinpress.com)
to order individual titles or the entire series.

DETECTING AND PREVENTING CLASSROOM CHEATING

PROMOTING INTEGRITY IN ASSESSMENT

GREGORY J. CIZEK

EXPERTS IN ASSESSMENT ™

SERIES EDITORS
THOMAS R. GUSKEY AND ROBERT J. MARZANO

CORWIN PRESS, INC.
A Sage Publications Company
Thousand Oaks, California

For information:

Corwin Press, Inc.
A Sage Publications Company
2455 Teller Road
Thousand Oaks, California 91320
www.corwinpress.com

Sage Publications Ltd.
6 Bonhill Street
London EC2A 4PU
United Kingdom

Sage Publications India Pvt. Ltd.
B-42 Panchsheel Enclave
Post Box 4109
New Delhi 110 017 India

Printed in the United States of America

Library of Congress Cataloging-in-Publication Data

Cizek, Gregory J.
Detecting and preventing classroom cheating : promoting integrity in assessment / by Gregory J. Cizek.
    p. cm. -- (Experts in assessment)
Includes bibliographical references and index.
ISBN 0-7619-4654-3 (Cloth) -- ISBN 0-7619-4655-1 (Paper)
    1. Cheating (Education) 2. Classroom management. I. Title.
II. Series.
LB3609.C48 2003
371.26--dc21

                                            2002155672

Acquisitions Editor:	Rachel Livsey
Editorial Assistant:	Phyllis Cappello
Production Editor:	Julia Parnell
Copy Editor:	Kristin Bergstad
Typesetter:	C&M Digitals (P) Ltd.
Proofreader:	Scott Oney
Cover Designer:	Tracy E. Miller
Production Artist:	Janet Foulger

Contents

Series Editors' Introduction

Standards, assessment, accountability, and grading—these are the issues that dominated discussions of education in the 1990s. Today, they are at the center of every modern education reform effort. As educators turn to the task of implementing these reforms, they face a complex array of questions and concerns that little in their background or previous experience has prepared them to address. This series is designed to help in that challenging task.

In selecting the authors, we went to individuals recognized as true experts in the field. The ideas of these scholar-practitioners have already helped shape current discussions of standards, assessment, accountability, and grading. But equally important, their work reflects a deep understanding of the complexities involved in implementation. As they developed their books for this series, we asked them to extend their thinking, to push the edge, and to present new perspectives on what should be done and how to do it. That is precisely what they did. The books they crafted provide not only cutting-edge perspectives but also practical guidelines for successful implementation.

We have several goals for this series. First, that it be used by teachers, school leaders, policy makers, government officials, and all those concerned with these crucial aspects of education reform. Second, that it helps broaden understanding of the complex issues involved in standards, assessment, accountability, and grading. Third, that it leads to more thoughtful policies and programs. Fourth, and most important, that it helps accomplish the basic goal for which all reform initiatives are intended—namely, to enable all students to learn excellently and to gain the many positive benefits of that success.

Thomas R. Guskey
Robert J. Marzano
Series Editors

Preface

Almost certainly, every educator has been touched by cheating in some way or another. If, as teachers or administrators, our backgrounds are like most of our students', at one or more times in our own education it is likely that we took a test or completed an assignment and were aided in some way that was not appropriate. Perhaps we failed to credit the work of others in a term paper; or maybe we just outright cut-and-pasted chunks of material from other sources and formatted that potpourri of information into "my" report. We may have copied from another student, passed or accepted a slip of paper containing information that should not have been given or received during a test. Maybe we claimed to be ill so that we might eke out an extra day or two to complete an assignment beyond the stated deadline.

Into our careers as educators, we have almost certainly experienced cheating from the other side of the desk. Perhaps it was the writing style used by a student in her term paper that was inconsistent with her previous work in the class. Maybe it was in observing one student looking intently in the direction of another student during a test and wondering whether he was attempting to copy an answer, or just innocently staring across the room. Perhaps it was in noticing that fifth-period Chemistry I students performed so much better on the quiz than first-period Chemistry I students did, even though both classes were taught the same material and given the same quiz. Maybe it was in the uncomfortable feeling accompanying rumors that a fellow teacher had provided "hints" to students regarding their answers to certain questions on the state-mandated mathematics test.

Whether in the form of tests, quizzes, portfolios, term papers, projects, or assignments, assessment of student learning has always been an essential feature of American education. So, too, has cheating. With the prominence of so-called "high-stakes" testing and educational accountability systems, the visibility, importance, and consequences of assessment have only increased in recent years.

Vigorous debate continues about whether the increase in student testing that is currently observed in K-12 education in the United States is a needed reform or a detriment to student learning. One thing is clear, however: Increased testing has been accompanied by more frequent and more visible incidents of cheating. And the phenomenon does not appear to be limited to cheating on large-scale, high-stakes tests. Cheating has become a fairly common occurrence when students take classroom tests or prepare term papers or other assignments.

The problem of cheating is not limited, however, to those who take tests or turn in term papers. Perhaps due to the use of high-stakes tests in student and educator accountability systems, cheating is increasingly committed by those who give tests.

The prominence of cheating has caught many educators, administrators, and policymakers by surprise. Confusion marks our ideas about what constitutes cheating. Uncertainty exists regarding how best to prevent cheating. Hesitance characterizes our notions of how to respond to cheating.

Despite apparent recent increases, cheating is not a new phenomenon. A little-known but solid body of research evidence and practical advice has accumulated over several decades to address the questions of what constitutes cheating and the steps teachers and administrators can take to reduce and respond to it.

This book provides a collection of no-nonsense information about cheating geared toward the practical needs of teachers, principals, school board members, and policymakers—in short, toward those who deal with the issue in K-12 classroom contexts. The first chapter provides a workable definition of cheating and describes how cheating is studied in educational contexts. The chapter also provides information on students' reasons for cheating, and documents some characteristics of students and classrooms that are associated with cheating. Chapter 2 presents data and rationales to support the idea that cheating is a serious problem, including information on the frequency and consequences of cheating. This chapter also provides insights into students' and teachers' perceptions of cheating.

Because a first step in responding to cheating is recognizing it, Chapter 3 provides a catalogue of specific methods used to cheat on tests and assignments. In Chapter 4, both traditional and more high-tech methods for detecting cheating are provided. Preventing cheating is the topic addressed in Chapter 5; this chapter includes practical suggestions for teacher actions and changes in classroom environments that can reduce the incidence of cheating. A concluding chapter, Chapter 6, suggests some next steps that will be of interest to educators and others who want to address the problem of cheating. Each chapter ends with several questions that can be used for individual reflection, or can serve as prompts for further group discussions.

Several resource sections are also included. Resource A is a glossary of key terms. Resource B provides a sampling of some Internet sources that aid students in cheating. Resource C is the counterpart to Resource B; it provides educators with an annotated list of some resources for combating cheating. Resource D includes examples of model cheating policies and honor codes. This book on cheating concludes with (naturally) a complete list of references used in preparing this work, and various indexes.

Before diving right into the subject of cheating, a few notes and acknowledgments are in order. First, I have written other books and articles on the topic of cheating, all of which have been of the densely footnoted, scholarly variety. Those works have also gone into considerably more depth than the present volume, and, for the reader whose interest in the subject of cheating is piqued, references to those previous efforts can be found in the list provided at the end of this book. Most of that previous work has focused exclusively on the specific problem of cheating on tests. While I obviously hope that the former works have been helpful to assessment specialists, those who oversee testing programs, policymakers, and so on, the present volume has a decidedly wider focus and a different audience in mind.

Compared to addressing a more academic audience, this book has given me the opportunity to write primarily for educators—an audience with whom I feel the closest affiliation. I began my own career in education as an elementary school teacher (2nd and 4th grades) for five years. After a stint in a testing organization, I returned to the classroom—though this time to the college classroom—and have now spent the majority of my career in a university setting. More than anything else, I still consider myself to be a teacher. So, when Tom Guskey (coeditor of the *Experts in Assessment*™ series with Robert Marzano) offered me the opportunity to contribute to this series for educators, I was both honored and delighted.

I have seized on Tom's offer as an opportunity to write in a different way. As readers will (I hope) notice, I have tried to avoid breaking up the text with citations. I have tried to write in a more conversational style, and to include more practical illustrations of the sort that I—and presumably many other teachers—have encountered in classrooms. I have omitted treatment of topics such as how to use simple statistical methods to detect cheating (readers can see my other writings for that topic), and I have included treatment of topics that I had not previously given much attention to, such as plagiarism and the emerging, high-tech methods that can be used to combat that form of cheating.

In addition to the series editors, I must also acknowledge the support and assistance of many others. First, some of what I know about cheating has been acquired via my own personal experiences as a student, teacher, and scholar. However, the vast majority of what I know about cheating is the result of encountering the work of other scholars who have labored tirelessly investigating the topic, and my own research and writing lean heavily on the shoulders of their efforts. A quotation from author Wilson Mizner seems appropriate to make the point: "If you steal from one author, it's plagiarism; if you steal from many, it's research."

Thus, proper attribution of the intellectual history that makes such a book as this possible must recognize many others. Several scholars who have devoted major portions of their careers to studying, understanding, preventing, or detecting cheating deserve recognition; among them, the significant contributions of Professors Fred Schab, Robert B. Frary, Stephen F. Davis, and John P. Houston warrant special mention. Studies of cheating are becoming somewhat rarer, however, as fewer young scholars commit themselves to the topic and apparently fewer resources are allocated to furthering an understanding of the issue and fostering academic integrity. Nonetheless, a few organizations persist in these efforts, most notably the Center for Academic Integrity at Duke University and the California-based Joseph and Edna Josephson Institute of Ethics. (Additional information on these organizations and others can be found in Resource C.)

In addition to the aforementioned intellectual assistance, I want to acknowledge the considerable editorial expertise and encouragement provided by Corwin Press, which has a long and successful history of publishing practical, helpful works in the field of education.

Finally, I am so grateful for the continuing support of my wife, Rita, and our children, Caroline, David, and Stephen, who I join in thanking God for showering his abundance on the American educational system and in pleading his continuing favor.

—GJC

About the Author

Gregory J. Cizek is Professor of Educational Measurement and Evaluation at the University of North Carolina at Chapel Hill. His background in the field of educational assessment includes five years as a manager of licensure and certification testing programs for American College Testing (ACT) in Iowa City, Iowa, and 12 years' teaching experience at the college level, where his teaching assignments have consisted primarily of graduate courses in educational testing, research methods, and statistics. He is the author of over 150 books, chapters, articles, conference papers, and reports. His books include *Handbook of Educational Policy* (1998), *Cheating on Tests: How to Do It, Detect It, and Prevent It* (1999), and *Setting Performance Standards: Concepts, Methods, and Perspectives* (2001).

Dr. Cizek has served as an elected member and vice president of a local school board in Ohio, and currently works with several states, organizations, and the U.S. Department of Education on technical and policy issues related to large-scale standards-based testing programs for students in Grades K-12. He began his career as an elementary school teacher in Michigan, where he taught second and fourth grade for five years.

Contact information:

Gregory J. Cizek, PhD
110 Peabody Hall
School of Education, CB 3500
University of North Carolina at Chapel Hill
Chapel Hill, NC 27599-3500

E-mail: cizek@unc.edu

Web: http://www.unc.edu/depts/ed/akh/facpgs2/gcizek.html

CHAPTER 1

What Do We Know About Cheating in the Classroom?

This chapter provides some of the "nuts and bolts" necessary to begin a consideration of **cheating.** To start, we must admit that it is not always clear what constitutes cheating. Thus, a first step is to develop a workable definition of that term. Next, although generalizing is to some extent both necessary and dangerous, we look at what the evidence suggests are the characteristics of students who cheat. We will be answering the questions of who tends to engage in cheating, why they do it, and how often cheating occurs. Finally, this chapter addresses the issue of perceptions of cheating—on the part of both students and their teachers—and investigates whether and to what degree those perceptions differ.

What Is Cheating?

Almost from birth, it seems that every person has some intuitive sense of what constitutes cheating. When I and my younger brother, Randy, were ages 6 and 4, respectively, I recall his protest when our mother gave me the candy bar and a knife to cut it into two pieces for us to share. It was apparently obvious to my brother that that system had the potential for unfair results; he was astute enough, however, to suggest that the person cutting should not get first choice of which "half" of the candy he wanted. As an adult observer of the 2002 Winter Olympics, I felt a sense of unfairness when I learned of the scandal involving ice-skating judges who rated competitors based not on their performance but on political deals that had been struck.

Almost certainly, readers of this book have different backgrounds and perceptions than those I have just related about myself. As teachers and administrators, we surely bring a diversity of expectations, values, and experiences to our work in the education profession. Nonetheless, although everyone's "fairness-meter" is probably calibrated a little differently, there are instances of academic dishonesty that, to one degree or another, cause our natural sense of injustice to be piqued.

The following paragraphs present some typical scenarios that could prompt concerns about cheating. As you read the following situations, take a moment to consider whether you believe each situation should be labeled "cheating" or not. Try using the following code: Place a plus sign (+) by those situations that you believe clearly represent cheating; use a minus sign (–) for those you believe do not constitute cheating; and use a wavy line (~) for situations that could go either way or for which you would want additional information.

> A student spends several hours searching the Internet for information on "Crustacean Overcrowding: The Growing Threat of Planktonic Hyperreproduction in Freshwater Lakes." Finding a ready-made essay on the topic, the student downloads and submits the paper for her biology term paper.

> A third-grade student's art-fair project is apparently more the product of his parents' efforts than of the student's.

> A teacher who is proctoring 250 high school juniors taking the SAT on a Saturday morning in the school cafeteria notices that the student who has signed in as "Mark Stein" is not the Mark Stein she knows from her British Literature class.

> For a high-stakes high school graduation test, two friends arrange to sit next to each other and, during the test, one of the students passes a slip of paper to his friend.

> A student obtains a perfect score on a French quiz because she had advance access to an answer key for the quiz taken from the teacher's desk drawer.

> A student turns in a writing assignment for her Current Events class that reads almost word-for-word identically to an article in a recent issue of *Reader's Digest*.

A teacher who is administering the *Iowa Test of Basic Skills* to her second-grade class gives several students who have been working hard a few extra minutes to finish the Language Arts test.

A mother is observed silently mouthing answers to her young child who is participating in a kindergarten screening event at the local elementary school.

A student is found to have **"razored"** out several important pages from a library resource, preventing other students from gaining access to the resource for a term project.

Before submitting the bubble sheets following administration of the state-mandated math test, a fourth-grade teacher notices that six students have made careless mistakes, so the teacher bubbles in the correct answers for the students.

Our internal fairness-meters may vary, as will the particular circumstances involved in a potential occurrence of cheating. Some of the preceding scenarios may have seemed to be egregious examples of cheating. Others may have seemed less serious. Others may appear to be perfectly appropriate. For still others, we may want additional information about the situation before being willing to categorize the event as improper or not. The diversity of these situations and our personal responses to them illustrates the complicated nature of the topic of cheating and the need to develop a concrete definition. The U.S. Supreme Court faced a similar situation when they struggled to develop a definition of obscenity. Ultimately, they expressed their exasperation over the task. According to Justice Potter Stewart, "I could never succeed in [defining it] intelligibly," but "I know it when I see it" (*Jacobellis v. Ohio*, 1964, p. 197).

However, the diversity of circumstances and of our values and perceptions also highlight the need for some workable, general definition of cheating. Because there are so many varieties of cheating, a highly specific definition won't suffice, and a more broadly applicable definition is desirable. Such a definition is both helpful and necessary for understanding cheating, for judging whether any particular behavior is improper, and for communicating our expectations about appropriate and inappropriate behavior to students, parents, and fellow educators. The following is a workable definition of cheating that should be applicable in most classroom contexts:

Cheating: Any action that violates the established rules governing the administration of a test or the completion of an assignment;

> *any behavior that gives one student an unfair advantage over other students on a test or assignment; or any action that decreases the accuracy of the intended inferences arising from a student's performance on a test or assignment.*

The preceding definition has at least three key salient elements. First, cheating violates some understanding of what constitute appropriate activities for completing a specific academic activity. Such an understanding is one that can reasonably be presumed to be held in common by all members of a school community. Second, cheating violates a sense of fundamental fairness in that it affords one or more students an unfair advantage in learning, grades, or opportunities that other students do not have. In this sense, cheating is similar to what is sometimes called *test bias*—a situation in which, on a given test, some students perform better than others of the same ability, level of content mastery, and so on, due to factors that are unrelated to what the test is attempting to measure. Third, cheating confounds the meaning that can be made from the student's performance on a test or assignment. Typically, we would like for the summary indicator of the quality of a student's work (i.e., the student's test score, term paper grade, rating for performing a skill, etc.) to clearly communicate something about that work. In this sense, cheating can be thought of as something that introduces "noise" or "pollution" into the communication process, resulting in a degradation of our ability to make, understand, communicate, or use that indicator.

Despite these refinements, the foregoing definition of cheating still requires some clarification. For example, what is meant by "the established rules"? Must the rules be explicitly spelled out for each test or assignment, or are there implicit rules that teachers and students understand apply to tests or assignments and that are assumed to be acquired in a common educational culture? And what is meant by the "intended inferences"? These are important issues and they are addressed in detail in Chapters 5 and 2, respectively.

For the present time, however, the preceding definition should provide enough information upon which to build a common conception of that term as we now turn our attention toward greater understanding of the characteristics of persons who cheat.

Who Cheats . . . and Why?

Answering the question "Who cheats?" is fairly easy. As we will see in the next chapter, cheating is ubiquitous at all levels of schooling. Nearly all research on the topic of cheating (that has used a definition of cheating similar to the one given in the previous section) reveals that nearly everyone has cheated at one time or another. It is possible, however, to see some distinctions when looking at patterns of cheating. For example, differences exist between K-12 students and college students. There are differences depending on the type of cheating (e.g., copying on a test vs. plagiarizing on an assignment). Also, the research indicates that some student characteristics are more strongly associated with cheating than others. Before beginning a review of some of these aspects of cheating, however, we will digress briefly to examine how cheating is investigated.

How Do We Know What We Know About Cheating?

Most commonly, when researchers want to know how often or in what ways students cheat, they simply ask. Major benefits of survey approaches include that they are usually less susceptible to ethical concerns (e.g., they do not involve deception); they are direct; they can be used on a large scale; and they are adaptable to various ages, grade levels, and subject areas. There are, of course, problems with the survey approach; namely, simple self-report surveys are frequently the most susceptible to inaccurate results. It is well-known that respondents are not always truthful when presented with surveys that ask them questions regarding sensitive, illegal, or socially unacceptable behaviors.

Cheating appears to be an exception to that generalization, however. With percentages of students who indicate that they have cheated nearing 90% in some surveys, it would appear that only a small proportion of respondents were reticent about admitting to the behavior. Of course, nearly all of the research on cheating has also provided respondents with the safeguards of anonymity and confidentiality, which likely contribute to the routinely large percentages of students who admit to cheating. At least one other element might also help explain the findings: As we will see later, cheating may be losing some of its stigma, and may be decreasingly viewed by respondents as sensitive, illegal, or socially unacceptable.

Although surveys that directly ask students if they have cheated, how often, and in what ways are common, other methods have been used, though less frequently. Some of the first studies of cheating were conducted by researchers who returned assignments to students in which a purposeful calculation error had been made, resulting in the student's being awarded a higher score than was actually achieved. Using this strategy, researchers defined cheating as occurring whenever a student failed to report the error. Though this research design was common in early studies of cheating, it has virtually disappeared, perhaps because it is unclear whether that behavior should even be considered to be cheating.

Another early—though remarkably sophisticated—method of estimating the incidence of cheating was described by Zastrow (1970). Working in a collegiate setting, Zastrow administered three two-page quizzes to students over the course of a semester. The first page of the quiz contained true/false questions, with a designated space for students to record their answers. All of the true/false questions were taken directly from the assigned textbook for the course. The second page contained an essay question. After completing the quizzes in class, students were instructed to separate the two pages. The essay responses on the second page were turned in for scoring by the instructor, but students were directed to take the first page home for self-scoring of the true/false questions.

Unbeknownst to the students, special materials were used to construct the pages of the two-page test. The back of the first page was coated with a unique substance that left an imperceptible record of the answers students marked for the true/false questions on the page they turned in containing the essay response. When the essay page was exposed to a certain chemical, the imperceptible marks became very visible indications of students' original answers to the true/false questions. Using this approach, Zastrow was able to estimate the incidence of cheating by comparing the scores based on the students' original responses to the true/false questions with the scores the students assigned following self-scoring.

More recently, some researchers have estimated the incidence of cheating by administering a "test" to students while a fake answer key is left in plain view and the testing room is left unattended. The extent of cheating is investigated by looking for instances of agreement between students' answers and those contained in the phony answer key.

Another common strategy for investigating cheating involves somewhat more elaborate deception. A test is administered, collected, and scored without making any marks on the students' answer sheets. The students' scores are recorded by the researchers. A teacher or other person who is knowledgeable about the research study returns the tests to the students and informs them that she did not have enough time to grade the tests, and that the students will need to score their own tests. When researchers use this strategy, cheating is deemed to have occurred whenever the known (i.e., previously recorded) scores for students differ from the scores students award themselves.

It should be pointed out that the preceding two strategies for investigating cheating are likely to yield different estimates of the incidence of cheating when compared with the data yielded by surveys. When a student makes use of an "unintentionally" displayed answer key or purposefully misgrades his or her own paper, that is a different form of cheating than copying or plagiarism.

A final approach to investigating the incidence of cheating relies on statistical methods. Basically, all statistical methods for investigating cheating involve searching for improbable similarities in two students' responses. The extent of similarity of responses is quantified and expressed as a probability that the similar answers were produced independently—that is, without cheating. A clear advantage of statistical methods for investigating cheating is that, in contrast to surveys, statistical methods do not rely on students' willingness to admit to cheating. Drawbacks to the use of statistical methods include the inherent inaccuracy in any probabilistic approach, and the fact that statistical methods can be used to detect only copying on tests consisting of select-format type items. For the interested reader, a considerably more detailed presentation of statistical methods can be found in Cizek (2001).

In conclusion, many strategies have been developed and used to study cheating. Surveys—that is, simply asking people about their cheating behavior—are by far the most prevalent approach. Fortunately, in terms of accuracy, survey techniques have a fairly good track record when it comes to studying cheating. One study on this issue is illustrative. Erickson and Smith (1974) gave a test to 118 college students under conditions that provided an easy opportunity to cheat, but also for researchers to determine who had cheated. Erickson and Smith found that 43% of the students took advantage of the opportunity to cheat. Going a step further, Erickson and Smith then surveyed the students and asked whether or not they had cheated. They found that students who cheated tended to indicate so in response to the survey. (Not surprisingly, they also found that no student who did not cheat said that he or she did.) Similar studies have tended to reach the same conclusion. Thus, we can have some confidence that self-reported cheating via survey techniques yields accurate estimates of how often the behavior actually occurs.

Variables Related to Cheating

Most of the research on cheating has focused on describing the characteristics of students who cheat. Most of that research has investigated cheating at the college level and many good reviews of the research are available (see, for example, Whitley, 1998). Comparatively less research has been conducted in elementary and secondary school contexts, but enough is known about cheating across the grades to yield some confident conclusions about the topic.

In this section, some of that evidence will be reviewed. However, an important caveat is in order before continuing. Nearly all of the information we have on the characteristics of students who cheat is what is called *correlational* evidence. A good understanding of how to interpret correlational evidence is essential to making appropriate conclusions based on the research.

Correlation is a statistical technique used to determine the strength of any relationship that might exist between two things (variables). Correlations can range from –1.0 to +1.0. Negative values indicate that high values on one of the variables tend to be associated with low values on the other variable. For example, suppose we had data for a large group of high school chemistry students on two variables: Days Absent and Final Grade in Chemistry. If we were to calculate a correlation, it is likely that there would be a strong, negative (i.e., close to –1.0) relationship between these variables. That is, students with *higher* days absent would tend to have *lower* grades and vice versa.

On the other hand, suppose we collected simple measurements on the same students on two other variables: the students' heights and their shoe sizes. If we calculated a correlation, it is likely that there would be a strong, positive (i.e., close to +1.0) relationship between these variables. That is, *taller* students would tend to have *larger* shoe sizes, and vice versa.

At this point, we can now consider a few of the cautions about correlations. First, correlations are almost never solidly at the extremes of –1.0 or +1.0. Most of the time, correlations are closer to the middle of that range, which is 0.0. The reason is that there are almost always exceptions to even the strongest relationships. For example, the strong, negative relationship between Days Absent and Grades in Chemistry is never likely to reach –1.0 because there will always be those students who are absent a lot (perhaps due to illness, etc.) but who nonetheless obtain high grades, due to their effort, motivation, or any number of other reasons. Similarly, the strong, positive correlation between height and shoe size is never going to be perfect (i.e., +1.0) because there will be people who don't fit the trend; that is, there will always be some tall people who have small feet and some short folks who have big feet.

So, Caution Number 1 when interpreting correlational evidence is that there are always exceptions to the general tendency represented by the correlation. Knowing, for example, that a student had a high number of absences does not necessarily guarantee that the student also earned a low grade. This caution is important for interpreting the correlational evidence about cheating. There may be a positive relationship between fraternity/sorority membership and cheating (in fact, there is). That *does not* mean, however, that a student who is a member of a fraternity or sorority is a cheater.

Caution Number 2 regarding correlations is that the size of the correlation matters. Correlations near the extremes (i.e., near −1.0 or near +1.0) indicate very strong relationships and very strong tendencies. Such correlations are also very rare. Most of the time in the social sciences we observe correlations much closer to zero. A correlation of 0.0 indicates that there is no relationship between the two variables.[1] Weak positive or weak negative correlations (say, near +.25 or −.25) are much more common than stronger ones. Weak correlations mean that the relationships between the variables are very slight, hard to detect, and that there are likely a large number of other variables that contribute as much or more to the relationship. For example, there is actually a very weak positive correlation between height and IQ (near .05). What do we do with such information? Almost certainly there are other factors that contribute to individual differences in height and intelligence, and it is likely that some other unidentified variable accounts for the relationship (e.g., prenatal nutrition). Thus, for the most part, the press might find such a correlation to be mildly interesting, and may even sensationalize the relationship to make a few-second blurb on a news program or in a magazine. Scientists would probably continue to speculate as to why even such a slight correlation exists. But, for the most part, people could probably (and safely) ignore the finding because the tendency is so weak.

This second caution is also important for understanding the characteristics of students who cheat. Like most other correlational evidence in the social sciences, the correlations calculated between some personal characteristic and incidence of cheating are usually quite modest. Again, this means that even any tendencies that are identified are usually weak ones. Some are, arguably, strong enough to warrant our attention; others are weak enough to be safely ignored.

Finally, a third caution has to do with the fact that even the strongest correlations do not directly indicate that one of the variables *causes* the other. For example, we don't necessarily know whether being absent a lot causes a student to have low grades, or whether students who are getting low grades just decide to skip classes more often. By extension, does being in a fraternity or sorority cause a person to be more likely to cheat, or are persons who are not as reticent about cheating more likely to join a fraternity or sorority? To be sure, sometimes we know that the direction of a relationship *must* be in a certain direction. For example, if we are looking at the relationship between a student's sex and the incidence of cheating, we may not be sure if being a boy or a girl *causes* a person to cheat, but we are certain that the relationship could not go in the other direction; that is, it is not possible that engaging in cheating caused a person to be a boy or a girl! The bottom line for caution number 3 is that we should always be vigilant about avoiding the impulse to jump to conclusions about direction of effect or causation.

Characteristics of Students Associated With Cheating

A handful of student characteristics have been included in nearly every study of cheating: these include the student's sex, previous grades/achievement, and age or grade in school. A number of studies have also addressed membership in a fraternity or sorority and the strength of students' religious beliefs. The following sections summarize some of what we know about the demographic and other student characteristics associated with cheating.

Sex. Of the student characteristics related to cheating, sex has been the single most-studied variable, and there is a fairly solid body of research from which to draw conclusions about any differences between the sexes in terms of cheating behavior. At the elementary school level, there appears to be little if any difference between boys and girls in their propensity to cheat. Though most of the academic research on cheating has involved college-aged populations, some evidence in studies involving younger children is relevant.

An early, classic study of cheating was conducted by Hartshorne and May (1928), who investigated whether very young boys and girls would be tempted to "peek" in order to be successful at a school-related task. They found no differences between boys and girls. Subsequent studies also found no differences between boys and girls at the second- and third-grade level (Coady & Sawyer, 1986), at the sixth-grade level (Krebs, 1969), and in a sample of sixth, seventh, and eighth graders (Anderman, Griesinger, & Westerfield, 1998).

By the time students leave elementary school, however, sex differences begin to appear. At the high school level, researchers have documented a somewhat greater incidence of cheating on the part of boys (Davis, Grover, Becker, & McGregor, 1992; Schab, 1969). Even one of the few studies to find more cheating by girls in elementary school (Feldman & Feldman, 1967) found that any greater incidence of cheating by girls disappears by the senior year of high school, when the incidence of cheating by boys becomes greater. Interestingly, one other study found that while boys may cheat more in general, girls admitted to cheating as much as boys when the motivation for cheating was helping another student (as opposed to getting better grades, etc., for themselves; Calabrese & Cochran, 1990).

In postsecondary settings, sex differences persist and, perhaps, increase. Because of the comparatively greater amount of research on cheating conducted at the college level, we can be fairly confident regarding the consistent finding of more cheating admitted by males (see Baird, 1980; Davis et al., 1992; Hetherington & Feldman, 1964). A study by Baldwin, Daughtery, Rowley, and Schwarz (1996) involving students at the high school, college, and graduate (medical school) levels also found greater incidence of cheating by males at each level.

In conclusion, a reasonable summary of the evidence regarding the relationship between sex and cheating is that there are essentially no differences between boys and girls in the early school years, but that boys surge ahead of girls in the later high school years and are consistently found to engage in cheating more than girls during college and beyond. Some of the most recent evidence suggests, however, that any post–high school "cheating gap" may be decreasing, though the reasons for decreasing differences between boys and girls are not yet clear. A number of speculations can be put forth for declining sex differences in cheating. As one researcher summarized the situation,

> This difference appears to be eroding, and some recent studies have reported similar rates of cheating for female and male students. Despite evidence that girls have a greater tendency to follow rules and fear of the consequences if they are caught, women may have a growing sense that they have to cheat to compete with the male students they see cheating in their classes. This tendency seems especially true at the college level in historically male-dominated majors such as business and accounting. (McCabe, 2001, p. 41)

Previous Grades/Achievement. A second commonly investigated student characteristic that has been studied for its possible relationship to cheating is students' previous academic achievement or course grades. Although there are, as usual, some exceptions, it seems to hold generally that students with weaker previous achievement tend to cheat more often than higher-performing students.

At the elementary school level, there is comparatively little research on the relationship between grades and cheating. However, one fairly large-scale study conducted in California elementary schools found more cheating by students with lower grades in a diverse sample of California elementary school students (Brandes, 1986).

At the college level, numerous studies have observed the tendency for cheating to be engaged in more frequently by students with weaker prior achievement. For example, Baird (1980) found a moderate negative correlation (–.34) between students' self-reported frequency of cheating and their self-reported grade point averages (GPAs). From the discussion of the concept of correlation presented previously in this chapter, we can interpret this finding to mean that there is a modest tendency for students with *lower* GPAs to admit to *more* cheating, and vice versa. A similar, negative correlation between cheating and grades was found by Antion and Michael (1983), who compared self-reported GPAs with actual (as opposed to self-reported) cheating in a group of community college students. Another study (Scheers & Dayton, 1987) found hefty differences in amounts of self-reported cheating for various GPAs, ranging from 21% of students at the highest GPA level admitting to copying on examinations to 86% at the lowest GPA level.

Overall, the research on the relationship between student ability and likelihood of cheating paints a fairly consistent picture. Students with lower prior achievement appear to be more likely to cheat; students with higher prior achievement are less likely. Our knowledge of how to interpret correlational evidence reminds us, however, that the relationship is only slight to moderate, and that having poor prior grades does not *cause* a student to cheat, nor do high grades inoculate a student against the temptation.

Age/Grade in School. A third commonly studied characteristic is students' age or grade level in school and its relationship to cheating. This relationship is somewhat more complex than the other variables we have looked at so far (i.e., sex, prior grades). This is because age or grade level *changes* while students progress through school while, for example, a student's sex remains the same. Further, as a student progresses through the grade levels, other factors can also change, such as the student's family structure, socioeconomic status (SES), achievement, maturity level, and so on. We know from other research examining these changes that, as a group, students tend to become more homogeneous in terms of achievement, more motivated, more economically advantaged, and (of course) older, as they progress through the American educational system.

These changes are probably obvious. However it is important to state them in light of the cautions for interpreting correlational evidence mentioned previously in this chapter. Namely, if (for example) cheating increases with the age/grade level of students and students tend to have greater levels of achievement motivation as they progress through the grades, then we cannot be sure from correlational evidence whether the increase in cheating should be attributed to simply getting older, or to increased achievement motivation (or both) or to some combination of these and other changes that occur as students progress through the grades.

For our purposes, we will not explore all of the nuances inherent in these relationships. There is sufficient evidence to arrive at some basic conclusions about the relationship between the age/grade level of students and the incidence of cheating. If graphed, the pattern would look like an inverted U shape. That is, cheating is comparatively scarcer in the early elementary grades, it reaches a peak in the late high school years, then it tapers off somewhat in college. First, I review some of the evidence that supports this conclusion. Then, as before, a few cautions will be mentioned.

There is abundant evidence that cheating appears to reach a peak in high school. For example, in Brandes's (1986) study of California 6th and 11th graders, a significantly higher incidence of cheating was reported by the high schoolers than the elementary school students. In the study by Davis et al. (1992), students self-reported significantly less cheating in high school than in college. In Baird's (1980) survey, 84.5% of the students reported cheating while they were in high school, whereas 75.5% reported cheating in college.

In summary, the relationship between cheating and student age/grade level is fairly sure. The primary caution when interpreting the evidence pertaining to student age/grade level and cheating is that the evidence is predominately of the survey or self-report variety. That means, for example, that we cannot be sure that cheating truly declines at the college level. It may be that college students cheat as much or more than high school students but are simply less inclined to *admit* to cheating. Such speculation is bolstered by the fact that, in many collegiate settings, the penalties for cheating can be considerably more serious than they generally are at the high school level. Even when it comes to data sources other than surveys, it is reasonable to ask whether there is really less cheating in college, or simply whether few students are caught. Another possibility is that, if cheating is related to achievement and those at lower achievement levels are more likely to cheat, those same students may be less likely to enter college in the first place.

Other Student Characteristics. A number of other student characteristics have been investigated for their potential relationship to cheating. Some of these characteristics have been investigated in great depth; some have received only slight attention. In Table 1.1 a potpourri of such characteristics is presented along with tentative classifications according to what the evidence indicates about its relationship to cheating. Rather than attempt to cover the landscape in great depth, characteristics will be identified along with a key study from which the finding was obtained and the context in which the research was conducted (e.g., elementary, secondary, college). It is important to note at the outset, however, that for many of these characteristics, the body of evidence is not as great as was the case for sex, previous achievement, or age/grade in school. Thus, these findings should be regarded with greater caution. The table organizes the characteristics into three groups: characteristics not associated with cheating; characteristics negatively related to cheating; and characteristics positively related to cheating. Again, we recall that a negative relationship indicates that "*more*" of some variable is related to *less* cheating and vice versa, while a positive relationship indicates that more of the variable is related to more cheating.

Conclusion. A review of Table 1.1 suggests that any conclusions about student characteristics related to cheating are not so tidy. The research probably confirms some stereotypes about cheating; other stereotypes don't appear to hold. Ascertaining which students cheat based simply on student characteristics is, for the most part, little better than guessing. (In fact, a study has even been conducted on this issue! In a study of high school boys' performance on a geometry test, the researchers found a modest but positive relationship between teachers' hypotheses about student cheating and the students' actual cheating on a self-graded test [Leveque & Walker, 1970]).

Information about some tendencies for certain student characteristics to be related to cheating may be interesting, but, as was noted earlier, these relationships provide only crude guidance at best. Overall, the best predictor of cheating on an assignment or test appears to be having cheated previously. The landmark study of cheating by Bowers (1964) found that 64% of students who reported cheating in high school went on to cheat in college; conversely, 67% of those who said they had not cheated in high school reported that they sustained academic honesty in college.

In summary, the evidence presented in Table 1.1 serves not so much as an aid to identifying student characteristics that predict cheating as it does as a caution about making improper generalizations and a stimulus to arranging student **assessments** in such a way as to prevent academic dishonesty.

Characteristics of Classrooms Associated With Cheating

Though comparative studies have not been done, it is almost certain that classroom factors—such as teacher characteristics, characteristics of the test or assignment, and classroom environment—have as much or more to do with cheating than student characteristics. In fact, surveys of students reveal that they commonly report classroom factors as being related to cheating. For example, in one survey in which college students were asked to identify the factors most

Table 1.1　Student Characteristics, Contexts, and Their Relationship to Cheating

No Relationship to Cheating	*Context*	*Reference*
Absence from class	College	Black (1962)
Achievement motivation	College	Roig & Neaman (1994)
Church membership	College	Knowlton & Hamerlynck (1967)
Conservative/liberal political beliefs	College	Clouse (1973)
Extracurricular activity participation	College	Baird (1980)
Minority/majority ethnicity	Grade 6-8	Anderman, Griesinger, & Westerfield (1998)
	Grade 9-12	Calabrese & Cochran (1990)
	College	Sierles, Kushner, & Krause (1988)
Moral reasoning/ development level	Grade 9-12	Bruggeman & Hart (1996)
Parental education level	Grade 6-8	Anderman, Griesinger, & Westerfield (1998)
Religious preference	College	Sierles, Hendrickx, & Circle (1980)
Self-esteem	Grade 5-6	Lobel & Levanon (1988)
Type A personality	College	Davis et al. (1992)

Negative Relationship to Cheating	*Context*	*Reference*
Academic self-concept	Grade 10-12	Rost & Wild (1994)
Being married	College	Diekhoff et al. (1996)
Church attendance	College	Hertherington & Feldman (1964)
Expectation of academic success	Grade 5-6	Vitro & Schoer (1972)
Intelligence (IQ)	Grade 9-12	Leveque & Walker (1970)
	College	Hoff (1940), Gross (1946)
Internal locus of control	College	Kahle (1980)
Introversion	Grade 6-7	Keehn (1956)
	College	Singh & Akhtar (1972)
Intrinsic motivation	Grade 5-6	Lobel & Levanon (1988)
Involvement in religious activities	College	Sutton & Huba (1995)
Learning orientation	College	Huss et al. (1993)

(Continued)

Table 1.1 (Continued)

Negative Relationship to Cheating	Context	Reference
Moral reasoning level	College	Leming (1978)
Need for achievement	Grade 10-12	Rost & Wild (1994)
Responsibility	College	Hertherington & Feldman (1964)
Self-support for college costs	College	Graham et al. (1994)
Trust in others	Grade 5	Doster & Chance (1976)

Positive Relationship to Cheating	Context	Reference
Alienation/dislike for school	Grade 9-12	Calabrese & Cochran (1990)
Arrests	Grade 9-12	Calabrese & Cochran (1990)
Belief that peers cheat	College	McCabe & Trevino (1993)
Chance of detection	Grade 6	Hill & Kochendorfer (1969)
	College	McCabe & Trevino (1993)
Cheating (engaging in one form of cheating)	College	Roig & DeTommaso (1995)
Cheating (previous cheating)	Grade 9-12	Bowers (1964)
	College/ Medical school	Baldwin et al. (1996); Sierles, Hendrickx, & Circle (1980)
Employment, full-time	College	Nowell & Laufer (1997)
Ethics instruction	College	Ames & Eskridge (1992)
Fear of negative evaluation	College	Dickstein, Montoya, & Neitlich (1977)
Felony conviction	College	Heisler (1974)
First-born child status	College	Hertherington & Feldman (1964)
Fraternity/sorority membership	College	McCabe & Bowers (1996)
Grade orientation	College	Huss et al. (1993)
Intramural athletics participation	College	Haines et al. (1986)
Intercollegiate athletics participation	College	Diekhoff et al. (1996)
Motivation to avoid failure	Grade 10-12	Rost & Wild (1994)
Need for approval	Grade 5-6	Lobel & Levanon (1988)

Positive Relationship to Cheating	Context	Reference
On-campus housing	College	Graham et al. (1994)
Procrastination	College	Roig & DeTommaso (1995)
Scholarship awardee	College	Diekhoff et al. (1996)
School anxiety	Grade 10-11	Shelton & Hill (1969)
	College	Antion & Michael (1983)
Socio-economic status (SES)	Grade 9-12	Leveque & Walker (1970)

related to frequent cheating, 42% said that "instructor shortcomings" were responsible, followed by characteristics such as the physical setting of the classroom (35%), and characteristics of the test or assignment (23%; Knowlton & Hamerlynch, 1967).

A number of specific relationships between classroom characteristics and cheating are presented in Table 1.2. The studies referenced in the table and others provide a somewhat clearer picture of school-related characteristics associated with cheating compared with the situation described previously for student characteristics.

Overall, the evidence suggests that students tend to cheat less often when

- Classes are smaller
- Classroom conditions (both physical and instructional) are established that are conducive to learning
- Instruction, assignments, and tests are clear, well-designed, meaningful, and relevant
- Teachers take reasonable steps to prevent cheating

Beyond these key conclusions, there are also some useful lessons to be learned from students and their perceptions of their teachers and classroom conditions. Two studies are particularly illuminating. In the first study, junior high school students were asked about the classroom variables they believed were most related to cheating. The students mentioned a number of classroom factors, but a large percentage of those surveyed (65%) indicated that "a lack of clarity about reasons or purposes for learning" was an element strongly related to cheating (Evans & Craig, 1990, p. 334). In the second study, Genereux and McLeod (1995) investigated the perceptions of college students related to cheating and classroom factors. One of their findings was that cheating was more likely when students perceived that their instructor assigned unreasonable amounts of work. More disconcerting,

Table 1.2   School and Classroom Characteristics, Contexts, and Their Relationship to Cheating

No Relationship to Cheating	Context	Reference
School type (public/private)	High school	Bruggeman & Hart (1996) (though Calabrese & Cochran [1990] found more cheating in private schools; McCabe [2001] found more cheating in public schools)

Negative Relationship to Cheating	Context	Reference
Course content meaningfulness/ interest	College	Steininger, Johnson, & Kirts (1964)
Instructional quality (student-perceived)	College	Blackburn & Miller (1996)

Positive Relationship to Cheating	Context	Reference
Class size	College	Nowell & Laufer (1997)
Coercive classroom management style	Grade 4-6	Houser (1982)
Distracting classroom environment	College	Houston (1976)
High performing schools	Elementary	Brandes (1986); Anderman, Griesinger, & Westerfield (1998)
	High school	Brandes (1986)
Opportunity to cheat	College	Cooper & Peterson (1980)

however, was the finding that many students reported that their teachers seemed unconcerned about cheating. A more recent and larger-scale survey of high school juniors confirms this finding. The study revealed that 47% of high school juniors say their teachers sometimes ignore cheating; 11% indicated that they believed that their teachers simply didn't care about the problem (McCabe, 2001).

Students' Reasons for Cheating

In contrast to the complexities and nuances of other aspects of cheating, the reason students give for cheating is simple and straightforward: They want a higher grade than they might have earned without cheating.

In the preceding section, we saw that students are more likely to cheat under certain classroom or instructional conditions, such as when they perceive an assignment to be unfair, or when they perceive that they have been subjected to an inordinate workload. It is important to be aware of these perceptions on the part of students because—if we are interested in deterring students from cheating—these factors are largely under the classroom teacher's control. As such, conscientious instructors can attempt to be more cognizant of the amount of work they assign, the relevance and interest level of what is taught, and of basic fairness in testing and grading.

On the other hand, it is also important to remember that correlational evidence regarding variables that tend to be associated with cheating is just that: the factors are *related*, not *causal*. Classroom correlates are related to cheating, but they are not the *reasons* students cheat—at least they are not the reasons students provide when asked why they cheat.

Decades of investigations into students' reasons for cheating still boil down to one fundamental reason: higher grades. The finding holds across grade levels, sexes, subject areas, and settings. Researchers have frequently surveyed students and obtained lists of different reasons, so we even have evidence bearing on which motivations are of greater and lesser importance to students. However, even in the diversity of reasons given by students, the common thread of higher grades always emerges.

In most cases, the primary reason of wanting higher grades even subsumes most of the other, less often stated reasons. For example, one of the earliest studies to elicit students' reasons for cheating was a simple, confidential survey of grade school and high school students (Ludeman, 1938). The researcher (who at the time was the dean of the Southern State Normal School in Springfield, South Dakota) published the survey and results in a school administrators' journal. An excerpt of the student questionnaire is shown in Figure 1.1.

As Figure 1.1 reveals, getting better grades was the second most frequently mentioned reason for cheating at both the elementary and high school levels. At both levels, the most frequently given reason was "to keep up with the Joneses." The students reported that they believed other students cheated and got by, which caused them to cheat. At first glance, this reason might seem to be more related to peer pressure

Directions:

As a problem in research work in educational psychology, we wish to find out the truth about cheating in school. Will you co-operate with us and please check this questionnaire? You may tell the exact truth because your check work will not be identified, for you do not sign your name.

		Number of Responses	
		Grade School	High School
Did you cheat in grade-school/ high-school tests?	Yes	78	144
	No	103	37
Why were you forced to cheat?			
a. to get better grades		28	51
b. work was hard and cheating helped me keep up		8	17
c. I was lazy so I cheated because I didn't always have my lessons		14	25
d. to spite the teacher		5	14
e. because others cheated and got by		37	69

From Ludeman, 1938, p. 45.

Figure 1.1   1938 Survey of Elementary and High School Students' Reasons for Cheating

than a desire to get higher grades. However, it is important to remember that acceptable grading practices in education have changed dramatically. At the time this study was conducted, the most common grading plan was to assign grades in a normative fashion—what is now sometimes called "grading on the curve." In a **norm-referenced** grading scheme, a student's grade depends as much on how other students perform as it does on the student's own performance. A good score on a test could translate into a poor grade if most of the other students obtained higher scores. Thus, it is clear that the leading reason for cheating given by students in the 1930s—"because other students cheated"—was really a statement about a concern for getting a higher grade (or at least one that maintained position relative to the grades other students obtained).

Dozens of other studies—and many recent ones—have confirmed that the primary reasons elementary and secondary school students give for cheating are related to the press for higher grades. A deeper look at the reasons students feel compelled to cheat for grades is also informative, however. For example, some studies have attempted to understand the source of students' press for higher grades. Among the commonly identified underlying causes are the following:

- Increasing parental pressure to perform
- The role that grades play in college admissions
- Perceived unrealistic complexity, challenge, or time requirements of assignments

One study interviewed students about their reasons and recorded the students' comments. According to the students,

"Marks are more and more necessary for college."

"Many teachers are unreasonable about assignments. If they are unfair and pile on the work, your have to cheat in order to survive."

"Some tests are unfair. They don't cover what you have learned."

"There is too much emphasis on the marks you get rather than what you know."

"Parents keep pushing. They are not satisfied with less than a B average." (Cornehlsen, 1965, p. 107)

As far as cheating in college, the same pattern of results has also been documented in surveys of why college students cheat. A 1941 study by Drake concluded that "the crux of the situation is the competition for marks" (1941, p. 420). And the situation has apparently not changed much since the time of that survey. A survey administered in the 1980s gave college students a list of eight choices and asked them to indicate their reasons for cheating. Students were permitted to check more than one reason, but the results were the same: 35% of students identified competition for grades as the primary reason for cheating; 33% said they cheated because they did not have enough study time; 26% said that an unmanageable workload was the reason (Baird, 1980). Business majors were much more frank in the reasons they gave; according to a survey, the students reported that "cheating required less effort and that it was perceived as the best way to get ahead" (Stevens & Stevens, 1987, p. 27).

Conclusions

In its most essential form, cheating can be defined as *any action that violates the rules that have been established for a classroom test or assignment.* Under this definition, however, we would not be concerned if a student were to violate the rules of a test by, say, using a #3 pencil instead of a #2, or if the student were to submit a term project using a 10-point font instead of the 12-point font stipulated by the teacher. As regards cheating, we mean by "the established rules" of a test or assignment those guidelines that are intended (1) to prevent one student from gaining an unfair advantage over others in terms of grades, opportunities, rewards, and so on; and (2) to promote accuracy in the meaning that students, teachers, parents, and others can make from a student's performance.

In this chapter, we also saw some of the ways that cheating has been studied. We reaped some of the benefits of that research, especially as regards what social scientists have discovered about the characteristics of students and classrooms that tend to be related to cheating. In short, many student characteristics are related to cheating, though most only modestly so. In the social sciences, it is axiomatic that the best predictor of future behavior is past behavior. As it turns out, the same is true for cheating: The best predictor of cheating on a current test or assignment is whether the student has cheated on a similar test or assignment in the past. As far as other student characteristics, the state of the evidence is such that it would be highly inappropriate—and inaccurate—to speculate about any particular student's likelihood of cheating based only on knowledge of any of the various characteristics that have been studied to date.

Student characteristics are also not something that teachers can do much (if anything) about. On the other hand, there are many classroom characteristics related to cheating and over which teachers have substantial control. Among these are teacher's classroom management style, the level of difficulty and amount of work assigned to students, and the fairness of tests and assignments. (In Chapter 5 we will take a closer look at these factors—and others—in an attempt to focus on how cheating can be prevented.)

Finally, in this chapter we learned about students' reasons for cheating. Surveys and interviews with students in elementary school, high school, and college have yielded very consistent findings. In brief, cheating is usually viewed as a time-saving way to get better grades. In an interview for the *Atlanta Journal-Constitution,* an elementary school student from Orlando, Florida, summarized her rationale for cheating: "Ten minutes of cheating is better than two hours studying" (quoted in Cumming, 1995, p. B2). A high school student participating in a focus group on cheating told the researcher, "If cheating is going to get you the grade, then that's the way to do it" (quoted in McCabe, 1999, p. 683).

All of the information about cheating presented in this chapter is not necessarily a cause for hand-wringing, however. For example, we might not be worried about cheating if no harm resulted from the behavior. Or, even if it were established that cheating was harmful in some ways, it might not be a cause for concern if it happened very infrequently. Thus, before concluding that cheating should receive greater or lesser attention in the classroom, it is important to ascertain how frequently cheating occurs and what harm, if any, it poses. We pursue these issues in the next chapter.

Questions for Further Discussion

Look again at the scenarios beginning on page 2. What other classroom situations have you encountered that

> You believe are clearly cheating, but some of your colleagues do not?

> You believe are not cheating, but some of your colleagues consider to be cheating?

> You are uncertain as to whether they represent cheating or not?

Consider the definition of cheating presented at the bottom of page 3. Do you agree with this definition? What parts of the definition would you change?

Perhaps you have heard a teacher say something like, "I just *know* that a student has cheated, but I can't prove it." Think of a time when you had such a feeling. What characteristics of the student or the situation do you think led you to feel that way?

Besides those mentioned in the chapter, what student, teacher, or school characteristics do you think (a) encourage and (b) discourage student cheating?

This chapter touched on some ways that researchers study cheating. If you wanted to investigate cheating in your classroom/school/district, what specific things might you do?

Note

1. For our purposes, this statement is accurate enough. However, a more technically precise rendering would note that a correlation of 0.0 means that there is no *linear* relationship between the variables.

CHAPTER 2

Why Is Cheating a Problem?

This would be a very short chapter if discussion of why cheating is a problem focused only on the simple fact that it is usually prohibited.

For many readers, the straightforward and sufficient answer to why cheating is a problem is that it is wrong. Actions that are wrong, proscribed, illegal, or otherwise formally sanctioned are classified as such because they transgress established rules, violate essential moral or ethical codes, cause harm to others, or degrade beneficial legal, social, political, or other institutions. Because cheating is a violation of established rules for academic behavior, it is, by definition, wrong.

But beyond this fundamental rationale for concluding that cheating is a problem are two other factors. First, cheating would not be as serious a problem if it occurred rarely. However, as we see in the next section, cheating is hardly rare. Second, even if widespread, cheating might not be considered problematic if the consequences of cheating were benign. In a final section of this chapter, I examine the results of cheating.

The Ubiquity of Cheating

A person is probably exaggerating if he or she proclaims, "But everybody does it!" when confronted about some misbehavior. However, cheating may in fact be an exception to this. Apparently everyone—or nearly everyone—really does cheat.

When questioned about how much cheating occurs, students are remarkably frank. The literature on cheating contains an abundance of anecdotes:

> It's almost a big deal if you *don't* cheat. (junior high school student, quoted in Bushweller, 1999, p. 26)

> Everybody does it . . . I don't feel guilty [about cheating]. I feel good because I'm going to get a good grade. (ninth-grade girl from Los Angeles, quoted in Levine, 1995, p. 66)

> If you don't, you're abnormal. (junior high school boy interviewed about the problem of fabricating data for student science fair projects, quoted in Bushweller, 1999, p. 28)

> I don't know if it's just our school, but like everybody cheats. Everyone looks at everyone else's paper. (student interviewed by McCabe, 1999, p. 683)

As it turns out, it's *not* just her school. Larger-scale surveys confirm the anecdotal conclusions of the students. For several years *Who's Who in American High Schools* has conducted such surveys. In 1996, they asked 3,351 college-bound high school students who had A or B averages about cheating: 89% said that cheating is "common" at their school; 58% reported that it was "easy" to obtain test questions or answers. Seventy-six percent admitted to having cheated themselves; 66% admitted to copying someone else's homework; 39% admitted to cheating on a test or quiz. It is perhaps important to note that, though high achievers, these students do not appear to be of the stressed-out-because-of-pressure-for-high-grades variety. Seventy percent of them reported that their school was only "somewhat" or "not very" challenging; 54% said that they spend seven hours or less a week studying (Who's Who Among American High School Students, 1996).

A follow-up survey two years later involved a different sample of 3,123 high school high achievers. The 80% of students who admitted to cheating was the highest percentage observed in the 29-year history of the survey. As in the previous survey, a high percentage of students (83%) indicated that cheating is common at their school, and 57% reported that advance copies of test questions or answers were not difficult to acquire (Who's Who Among American High School Students, 1998).

The recent surveys also reveal that cheating is clearly on the increase. One researcher has conducted surveys of college-level cheating at ten-year intervals since 1969. His findings include, for example, that the percentage of students who admit using a cheat sheet on tests increased from 34% to 68% over the years 1969–1989. Over the same period, the percentage of students who indicated they had plagiarized material for an assignment rose from 67% to 76%, and the percentage who admitted letting other students copy rose from 58% to 98% (Schab, 1991).

Other surveys have asked students about the frequency with which they engage in specific cheating behaviors. The results of one such study conducted by Brandes in 1986 are shown in Table 2.1. The survey was based on 1,037 elementary school students and 2,265 secondary school students enrolled in California public schools. The students' teachers ($n = 109$) were also surveyed.

Results consistent with Brandes's findings were found in a more recent survey of 2,294 high school juniors who were asked about specific cheating behaviors (McCabe, 2001). Table 2.2 reveals that the incidence of specific types of cheating remains high.

A few conclusions can be made based on these student reports about cheating. One is the dramatic difference shown in Table 2.1 between reported cheating in elementary and in secondary school. For example, while 15.4% of elementary students reported that they copied from another student during a test "a few" or "many" times, that number is 60.3% for high school students. Similarly, the percentages for use of cheat sheets are 10.0% and 57.1%, respectively; for the question addressing plagiarism, the percentages were 15.8% and 32.4%, respectively. Somewhat humorously, it seems that the only inappropriate behavior high school students report doing less often than elementary school students is "turning in work done by your parents."

As the table and the large body of other research demonstrate, fairly large percentages of students report engaging in a variety of cheating behaviors *in general;* that is, students tend to admit to specific behaviors in response to the basic question, "Have you done . . . ?" However, we have comparatively little hard data regarding the incidence of cheating on *any particular* assignment, project, test, or the like. That is, we are less sure about the percentage of students that are likely to cheat on the specific upcoming quiz or science project in *your* class.

Of course, there are a number of factors that contribute to the probability that cheating will occur in a specific situation, and we look at some of these in a subsequent chapter. But one or two bits of information give hints as to the percentage of students that are likely to be

Table 2.1 Self-Reported Cheating by Elementary and High School Students, 1986

Question:
Since you have been at this school, have you ever. . .

	Percentage of Elementary/ High School Students Indicating		
	Never	*One Time*	*A Few or Many Times*
– Seen another student cheat during a test?	14.3/ 3.3	15.7/3.8	70.1/92.8
– Used crib notes/cheat sheet during a test?	72.3/26.5	17.7/16.4	10.0/57.1
– Copied from another student during a test?	61.5/25.0	23.2/14.7	15.4/60.3
– Copied something word-for-word out of a book and turned it in as your own work?	58.7/49.2	25.4/18.4	15.8/32.4
– Copied from someone's paper without his or her knowing it?	73.5/55.3	17.2/15.6	9.3/29.0
– Arranged with other students to give or receive answers by use of signals?	84.2/62.5	8.4/13.7	7.5/23.8
– Used unfair methods to find out what was going to be on a test before it was given?	83.1/58.4	7.2/15.7	3.8/25.8
– Turned in homework another student did?	87.3/65.4	7.8/11.2	4.8/23.4
– Turned in work done by your parents?	86.4/90.8	8.8/4.5	4.8/4.6

Adapted from Brandes (1986, pp. 13, 16).

engaging in some prohibited behavior on this week's homework assignment or in-class quiz.

One intriguing study was conducted by specialists in library and information sciences who wanted to investigate the percentage of 11th-grade students in two schools who plagiarized information for a

Table 2.2 Self-Reported Cheating by Public High School Juniors, 2001

	Percentage of High School Juniors Indicating One or More
Cheating on Tests/Exams	
– Copied from another student on test/exam	66
– Used crib notes during a test/exam	45
– Got questions/answers from a student who had already taken the test/exam	75
– Helped another student cheat on a test/exam	62
Cheating on Homework/Plagiarism	
– Copied almost word-for-word and submitted as own work	37
– Copied a few sentences without citation	63
– Submitted work copied from another student	75
– Allowed another student to copy homework	90
– Submitted a paper obtained from a Web site or "paper mill"	18
Other	
– Worked on an assignment with other students when prohibited	77
– Turned in an assignment done by parent(s)	21

Adapted from McCabe (2001, p. 40).

research paper assignment (McGregor & Streitenberger, 1998). Forty-five students from three classes—one English class in Texas, and two classes (one English, one Social Studies) in Alberta, Canada were studied. As part of the directions for the assignment, all students were told that copying unattributed material from a source—that is, **plagiarism**—was prohibited, although, as part of the study, the Texas students were given much more detailed information about the issue of plagiarism and instruction on proper citation of source material.

The extent of plagiarism was measured via a straightforward approach of comparing the students' final papers with the material found in the sources listed in the bibliographies of the students' papers. Two aspects of plagiarism were examined. First, the researchers calculated the *amount* of each student's paper in which some type of plagiarism occurred. These codings ranged from Level 1 (no copying) to Level 5 (50% or more of the paper was copied). Second, different *kinds* of plagiarism were defined:

Table 2.3   Plagiarism in High School English Classes

Extent of Plagiarism *(Percentage of Paper Copied)*	*Alberta, Canada, English Class*	*Texas English Class*
Level 1 (no copying)	31%	50%
Level 2 (1-14%)	22%	40%
Level 3 (15-29%)	16%	0%
Level 4 (30-49%)	13%	5%
Level 5 (50% or more)	19%	5%

Note: Entries in the table are percentages (rounded) of Types D and E plagiarism (combined). Adapted from McGregor and Streitenberger (1998, Appendix A).

- Type C Plagiarism was defined as appropriation of major portions of text with significant word changes, but with identical structure for sentences and paragraphs.
- Type D plagiarism consisted of near word-for-word copying, but with minor changes in wording, verb tense, and so on.
- Type E plagiarism was defined as word-for-word copying.

The results are shown in Table 2.3. The amounts of word-for-word copying in both of the English classes seem fairly high. For example, approximately 10% of the Texas class and 32% of the Canadian class produced papers with 30% or more of their content consisting of unattributed, copied material. On the other hand, also of interest is the large percentage of students in the Texas class whose papers were free of plagiarism, or nearly so. This finding highlights that, when students are given specific warnings about plagiarism and instruction in proper citation, the incidence of this type of cheating can be diminished.

There is one other piece of evidence on the amount of cheating that can be expected on a specific occasion. Bellezza and Bellezza (1989) developed and applied a statistical method for detecting cheating on multiple-choice tests at the college level. Their method was designed to identify only one type of cheating: that involving two students who are seated next to each other during a test and who produce identical patterns of correct and incorrect answers to multiple-choice questions (i.e., copying). Summarizing over a variety of classes, they estimated the percentage of students who cheat on a specific occasion to be approximately 5%.

Conclusions About the Frequency of Cheating

Several conclusions can be drawn about the ubiquity of cheating. First, students seem to be telling the truth: Nearly everyone does cheat.

There is, of course, a broader context to cheating, and we should not lose sight of the fact that it's not just students who are doing it. As I write this chapter in the middle of the month of April, I wonder about the ubiquity of cheating as the deadline for filing U.S. income taxes approaches.

In another source, I have chronicled the incidence of cheating in a variety of occupations and cultures (Cizek, 1999). A recent article in *USA Today* described what is euphemistically called "sermon sharing" among ministers. Apparently there is a growing problem of some pastors preaching previously published passages as if the sermons were the result of their own preparation. The rabbi who wrote the *USA Today* article described plagiarism of his own work, as well as other examples of the trend. Among the cases cited was that of Reverend Edward Mullins, a minister in the suburban Detroit area who is currently under suspension while an investigation addresses allegations that his sermons and writings in a church newsletter were copied verbatim from various Web sites (Zelizer, 2002).

Thus, our first conclusion about the incidence of cheating is that, while every student (or at least close to every student) has probably engaged in cheating, they are not alone. We cannot escape the suggestion that cheating by students in school settings is perhaps just one manifestation of a broader cultural issue.

Second, cheating is not limited to the least-able students who, for example, might be inclined to cheat just to pass a class. When asked, "What type of students are more likely to cheat?" only modest percentages of the elementary teachers (5.7%) and high school teachers (27.0%) who responded to Brandes's (1986) survey identified high-achieving students. However, as the *Who's Who* surveys revealed, cheating is as pervasive—if not more so—among what are sometimes thought of as the best students; that is, those with good grades, intent on attending college, and so on.

Third, more cheating appears to be associated with certain contexts. For example, more cheating takes place at the high school level than in grade school classrooms. More cheating takes place on independent or less formal assignments (e.g., term papers, science fair projects, etc.) than on more formal assessments (e.g., supervised, in-class examinations). In a subsequent chapter, I consider these contexts and how educational settings and practices can be organized to minimize the likelihood of cheating.

Finally, as a number of longitudinal studies attest, the incidence of cheating appears to be on the rise. As one researcher summed it up,

> The evidence is unequivocal. The problem [of cheating] starts early and increases as students move through school. It has also

increased significantly at almost every level of our educational system in the last few decades. (McCabe, 2001, p. 38)

Several factors may account for the rise and ubiquity of cheating: among them, increasing competition for grades, high-stakes examinations, and an increasing acceptance of cheating as socially acceptable. These factors are considered in more detail in Chapter 5.

First, however, having some evidence in hand that cheating is not a trivial matter in terms of its frequency, we turn to a brief examination of some of its consequences.

The Consequences of Cheating

The consequences of cheating—both seen and unseen—is the second element that bears on the question of whether cheating is a problem. At first blush, it might seem like too much ado to invoke "more fundamental moral or ethical codes" in the context of one student flashing a hand signal to another student that "2" is the correct answer to the test question, "What is the cube root of 8?" It's not likely that failing to cite material cut-and-pasted from the Internet for a term paper is going to do measurable harm to great social institutions. Admittedly, in comparison to the vexing ethical concerns of the day—cloning, abortion, discrimination, poverty, capital punishment, and so on—peeking at a crib sheet is hardly a blip on the radar.

Even in the narrower context of important educational issues, it is difficult to argue that cheating should be the most serious concern on educators' minds. Good arguments can be made that attracting and retaining qualified teachers and administrators, maintaining safe and orderly learning environments, garnering adequate classroom resources, implementing challenging curricula, promoting high levels of parental involvement, and ensuring equal access to educational opportunities are all more pressing than addressing cheating.

Those caveats notwithstanding, cheating is still a serious problem, and one that should concern all involved in the educational process—students, parents, teachers, administrators, and policymakers—to the extent that results of cheating introduce negative consequences that affect these groups and society more generally. In addition to the straightforward reasons why cheating should be a concern, there are many other aspects, results, and effects of cheating that are rarely recognized. When the combined influence of these elements and the ubiquity of the behavior are considered, cheating can be seen as something considerably more harmful than it may have seemed at first blush. The following sections address the somewhat abstract social consequences of cheating, followed by the more practical consequences for students, teachers, and policymakers.

Social Consequences of Cheating

A number of writers have hinted at or spoken forcefully about the greater harm represented by cheating and the failure of educators to attend to it. According to Michael Josephson, founder and president of the Character Counts! Coalition and the Josephson Institute of Ethics, cheating is akin to "a hole in the moral ozone." In a radio address transcript posted on the Character Counts! Web site, Josephson stated,

> Some people, including a disturbing number of educators, dismiss [findings of widespread cheating] on various grounds such as: this generation is simply more honest about it's [sic] cheating, the cheater only hurts himself, and, cheating is an understandable response to the unwarranted pressure students feel in a system based on competition and grades. . . . [However], it's a great mistake to understate the significance of cheating in schools. Cheating is habit-forming. It becomes a way to cope with any situation where we want something we haven't earned or shouldn't have. So cheating leads to cheating. (Josephson, 1998, p. 2)

Other leaders involved in promoting character education in U.S. schools have voiced similar concerns, and suggested that cheating in school settings poses greater questions about society. According to one,

> Cheating is habit forming. Students who cheat in class may well cheat in their jobs or on their spouses. When you have a country that doesn't value honesty and thinks character is unimportant, what kind of society do you have? (Mulkey, quoted in Levine, 1995, p. 70)

Finally, Nancy Cole, a former president of Educational Testing Service (ETS), has also written about the broader social concern raised by cheating in education contexts. In a *USA Today* article, she noted that "cheating undermines integrity and fairness at all levels. It leads to weak life performance. It undermines the merit basis of our society. Cheating is an issue that should concern every citizen of this country" (1998, p. A-24). To the extent that cheating learned or reinforced in school settings is related to a person's subsequent occupational or civic performance, Cole's assertion demands the attention of educators.

Cheating and Accurate Information About Students

From a more pragmatic perspective, cheating is also problematic. In Chapter 1, a definition of cheating was provided that contained three elements: (1) a violation of what constitutes appropriate activities for completing a specific academic activity; (2) affording an unfair advantage in learning, grades, or opportunities; and (3) a reduction in the accuracy of inferences, meaning, or quality of communication about student performance. It is the second and third parts of the definition that encompass some of the most troublesome consequences of cheating and that warrant more thorough explication.

It is perhaps appropriate first to be clear about what is meant by *inferences,* as the notion of inferences is central to modern ideas concerning valid assessment.

According to the professional standards that apply to student assessment activities, *validity* is the single greatest concern (American Educational Research Association [AERA], American Psychological Association [APA], National Council on Measurement in Education [NCME], 1999). **Validity** refers to the accuracy of the inferences about student characteristics, usually based on observations of the student's performance—such as a test score, a term paper, or a lab experiment. The "inference" is the interpretation, conclusion, or meaning that a teacher *intends* to make about a student's knowledge, skill, or ability from the student's performance.

In nearly all cases, teachers purposefully design or choose an assessment to permit such inferences. Thus, a composition teacher would be inclined to interpret a well-crafted term paper as evidence that a student is a thoughtful and well-organized writer. A mathematics teacher would be likely to conclude that a student who correctly adds 20 out of 20 mixed numerals with different denominators has solid mastery of that process.

Unfortunately, the inferences a teacher *wants* to make are not always the inferences that *can* be made, and our conclusions about students are not unambiguous. It is a truism: The inferences we can make about a student's ability are necessarily tentative because we almost never have all of the evidence that would be necessary to proclaim our inference to be a fact.

For example, if the term paper were the product of more parental than student reflection, or more the result of cut-and-pasted organization from an Internet source than of the student's own writing skill, then the inference that the student has strong writing ability would be sketchy. If the perfect performance in adding fractions were the result of copying from another student, then the inference of "solid mastery" may simply be incorrect.

Phrased in only slightly more technical terms, we can see that validity is the degree to which all of the available evidence supports the inferences we wish to make about a student's knowledge, skill, or ability based on his or her observed performance. By definition, inferences are based upon a less-than-ideal amount of information, such as in the sample of a student's knowledge obtained via a single test or the sample of student research and writing skill obtained via a single term paper. Because it is often too costly or impractical to gather more information, we are forced to accept the fact that inferences *must* be based on samples of behavior. As a result, we are also compelled to admit the necessity of considering the accuracy of our inferences whenever they are based on a limited body of available evidence. That is, we must consider validity.

These ideas of validity as accuracy-of-inferences and sufficiency-of-evidence are central to modern test theory and are the foundation of professionally defensible assessment practice. Any factor that hinders a teacher's ability to make accurate inferences from the sample of performance threatens validity and jeopardizes the meaningfulness of conclusions about the test taker. To tie it all together: When cheating occurs, inaccurate inferences result.

"Inaccurate inferences" is not simply a concept without consequence, and we now turn to some examples of those consequences.

Practical Consequences for Students

One practical consequence of cheating is that it can result in inaccurate information about students. For example, consider the situation of so-called "grading on the curve." Although grading on the curve is not uniformly endorsed by testing specialists, it is still common practice in many schools. Under such a system, preestablished percentages of students are assigned the various grades. For example, a teacher (or school policy) might decide a priori that 5% of students will be awarded As, 15% will be given Bs, 50% Cs, 15% Ds, and 5% Fs. Thus, it is not only how much a student learns that affects his or her grade, but also how well the student performs *in relation to the other students*.

Under a system in which students are graded "on the curve," cheating introduces unfairness for those who *don't* cheat. Cheating by some students results in students who *did not* cheat being assigned *lower* grades than they would have otherwise. A student from North Springs High School in Fulton County, Georgia, summarized the problem. According to the student,

Seeing kids cheat . . . is especially frustrating when a teacher is grading students on a bell curve. Cheaters skew the curve, making it tougher for kids who don't cheat to get one of the higher grades. (cited in Bushweller, 1999, p. 29)

Ironically, there is little doubt that many honest students who received a lower grade because of cheating have actually been punished twice: first by being assigned an inappropriately low grade, then perhaps by a residual penalty such as being grounded by parents, missing the honor roll, losing a scholarship, and so on.

There is another practical consequence for students—at least as seen from the perspective of their teachers. Cheating may have become so commonplace that, like the high school student above, it is perceived that it is a disadvantage *not* to cheat. For example, a group of 51 Advanced Placement (AP) students were interviewed about their experiences with cheating. After the students confided to the interviewer regarding their frequent cheating, the interviewer

asked their teacher how he could tolerate such widespread cheating. The shocking explanation: "If we stopped our students from cheating, they would be at a competitive disadvantage [for college admissions]." (cited in Levine, 1995, p. 67)

A final example of practical consequences is the effect on students when others cheat on their behalf. One notorious recent case illustrates this point. The case involved a "boy genius," Justin Chapman, who at age six was reported to have an IQ of 298 as measured by the *Stanford-Binet Intelligence Scale,* and obtained a combined SAT score of 1,450—a perfect 800 on the math section and 650 on the verbal portion. The boy became world-famous—enrolling in college courses, speaking at conferences for gifted children, and being featured in newspaper and television programs about the child prodigy. A psychologist who administered the *Stanford-Binet* to Justin proclaimed him to be "the greatest genius to ever grace the earth"; Justin's mother, Elizabeth Chapman, believed that her son's performance had "opened a lot of doors for Justin" (quoted in Poppen, 2002, p. B-1).

In March 2002, however, Ms. Chapman revealed that her son's performance on the tests had been the result of cheating. She admitted that she had obtained a copy of the *Stanford-Binet* and coached Justin on it before he was administered the test. She also admitted that she had altered a copy of another student's SAT score report, substituting Justin's name for the student who had obtained the high scores. The consequences for Justin, now age eight, had become severe: his mother's admissions were the result of Justin's being hospitalized following an apparent suicide attempt.

In summary, the practical consequences of cheating for students are real and can be serious. Clearly, cheating such as that illustrated in the case of Justin Chapman is not common, nor are the consequences of cheating usually as severe. Nonetheless, Justin's story highlights the emotional and physical impact that cheating can have on students when inappropriate pressures or expectations result. Other practical effects of cheating include that it can impair our ability make appropriate educational plans for a student; it can result in frustration for students or teachers when students are mistakenly put in situations that require too great or too little an academic challenge; it can result in benefits being denied to more deserving students, as in competitive situations such as for scholarships or awards.

Consequences for Educational Systems

In addition to direct consequences for individual students, cheating also introduces undesirable consequences for schools and schooling systems. As one example, it is easy to see how widespread cheating could result in educational administrators or policymakers mistakenly concluding that innovations had been successful in raising student achievement.

Perhaps the most serious consequence of cheating, however, is the ephemeral effect it can have on the classroom. The intangible but damaging consequence of cheating is the erosion of the respect, trust, sense of community, and even student motivation for learning that can result.

For example, consider the case of a take-home test given at the end of the semester to an American History class. The teacher has given very explicit instructions regarding the test: Students may not use any books or notes; they must complete the test at home, independently; and they must not spend more than two hours working on it. After turning in her test, a student who followed the teacher's rules learns that nearly all of her classmates spent as much time they needed to complete the test and made liberal use of their books, notes, and even classmates to help with answers to the questions.

What effect might the classmates' cheating have on the student's likelihood of cheating in the future? What might be the effect on her perception of the goals of learning and assessment? What might be the effect on how she views the trust she can place in her classmates? What could be the effect on how she views the teacher's authority or her obligation to respect the teacher's guidelines in the future? What effect might learning of the cheating have on the teacher's future assignments and teaching practices, and on his respect for and trust in his students?

To be sure, these questions relate to potential effects on the individual student and teacher involved. More importantly however, they also bear the broader culture of the school and the educational system. It may be impossible to quantify these broader effects, but the impact on classroom climate, student-teacher and student-student relationships, and on perceptions about the aims of education, the means of success, and the meaning of achievement is a serious concern.

Students' and Teachers' Perceptions of Cheating

Previous sections of this chapter have looked at the frequency and consequences of cheating. The conclusions: Cheating occurs too frequently to ignore, and it has the potential to inflict harm across the range of those affected—from individual students and teachers, to educational systems, to the broader society. There is one final component to the problem that compounds the issue of addressing cheating—the problem of incongruent perceptions.

A disconnect in perceptions exists between those who cheat (primarily students) and those whose responsibility it is to monitor and address the problem (primarily teachers). The disconnect is characterized by the differing perceptions that students and teachers have about the frequency and consequences of cheating. If, to be simplistic, students cheated a lot, and if teachers recognized the extent of the problem and were committed to actions aimed at addressing it, a disconnect would not exist. By and large, however, teachers and students see the elements of the problem very differently. It is illustrative to contrast the perceptions of cheating expressed by a professor and a student, collected during interviews at the Massachusetts Institute of Technology (MIT):

> Professor: "I think you should bear in mind that many students—I hope and believe most—would never dream of cheating no matter what the pressures, opportunities or incentives."
>
> Graduate Teaching Assistant: "Copying is so common at MIT. I think students even forget that it is cheating." (quoted in Lispon & McGavern, 1993, p. 4)

There is plenty of other evidence that a difference in perceptions exists—one that likely contributes to the lingering prominence that cheating plays at all levels of schooling. The disconnect has several facets: Teachers and students have very different notions about what constitutes cheating; they have very different perceptions about how much cheating goes on; they have very different perceptions about the

Table 2.4   Students' Perceptions of Cheating

Question: "How would your classmates feel if a student cheated on a test?"

Answers	Percentage Choosing — Elementary School	Percentage Choosing — High School
Most would care very much	25.5	3.2
Most would dislike it a bit	35.6	21.6
Most would not care	38.9	75.3

amount of cheating that is detected; and they have very different levels of concern about the problem. Finally, students appear to talk among themselves about cheating; it seems that their instructors rarely do.

Perceptions About the Seriousness of Cheating

To begin with, by the time they reach high school, most students appear to believe that cheating is "no big deal." In fact, in the 1998 *Who's Who* survey, 53% of the high school students said exactly that: Cheating was "no big deal" (p. 2). Students in the California survey of elementary and high schoolers were asked how their classmates would feel if a student cheated on a test. Of the choices they were provided, a plurality (38.9%) said that most of their classmates wouldn't care. By high school, a sizable majority (75.3%) said that their classmates would have an apathetic response (see Table 2.4).

The "perception gap" was highlighted in a recent study in which students and their teachers were asked their perceptions about whether a specific behavior constituted cheating and how serious an infraction the behavior was (McLaughlin & Ross, 1989). The students and their teachers, drawn from a high school in Tennessee, were asked to indicate whether an action was or was not cheating, and to rate the severity of the listed action on a scale from 1 (not serious) to 5 (very serious). The results are shown in Table 2.5. As the table illustrates, students uniformly are less likely to judge specific behaviors as cheating compared with their teachers, and the students consistently view the behaviors as less serious. And the perception gap extends beyond MIT professors and their students, high school teachers and their pupils. According to the *Who's Who* (1998) survey, 63% of parents surveyed asserted that their children had never cheated; 11% said they had no idea if their student had cheated.

Table 2.5   Students' and Teachers' Perceptions of Cheating

Behavior	Percentage Classifying Behavior as Cheating		Rating of Seriousness of Behavior	
	Students	Teachers	Students	Teachers
* Copying during an examination	99	100	3.6	4.8
* Finding a copy of an exam and using it to study	79	100	2.9	3.6
* Arranging to give or receive signals during a test	95	100	3.1	4.3
* Looking at notes during a test	92	100	3.3	4.5
* Getting answers from someone who has already taken a test	74	90	2.4	3.5
* Asking someone for test answers	95	100	2.8	3.4
* Allowing another student to copy	87	100	3.2	4.4
* Copying an answer left by mistake on the chalkboard	30	50	1.6	1.8
* Giving someone an answer during a test	87	100	2.8	4.5

Note: Adapted from McLaughlin and Ross (1989).

Conclusions

A number of aspects related to the problem of cheating are fairly clear. For one, cheating appears to be a ubiquitous phenomenon at just about every level of schooling. Second, although cheating has probably occurred and probably will occur as long as there are tests, assignments, and grades, the evidence indicates that the problem is not getting any better. It is likely getting worse. Third, cheating is not a victimless crime. Its consequences touch those who cheat, those who do not cheat, and the educational communities in which students and their teachers are joined in pursuit of learning—academic as well as social and moral learning. The effects of cheating also extend beyond the borders of classrooms, having an impact on the broader society.

Fourth, there is a perception gap among pupils, parents, and educators regarding the frequency and seriousness of cheating.

In sum, it is almost impossible to conclude that cheating is not a problem. Addressing the problem entails several prongs; the first step for educators is being able to identify cheating, which is the topic of the next chapter.

Questions for Further Discussion

What is your reaction to researchers' survey and interview findings in which students say that they think cheating is "no big deal," that "everybody does it," and that "if you don't cheat, you're abnormal"? What do you think students at your school would say about cheating if they were interviewed?

How common do you think cheating is . . .

In your classroom?

At your school?

In your school district?

Do you think cheating is more or less common at your school than at others? Why?

Some people might say that cheating is a "victimless" crime. What do you think are the consequences of cheating on . . .

A student who cheats?

Other students in the classroom?

Education systems and society?

Do you think that students and teachers at your school generally agree on the frequency, seriousness, and consequences of cheating? Why or why not?

CHAPTER 3

How Does Cheating Occur?

This chapter represents a turning point. Previous chapters have (1) provided a definition of cheating; (2) documented the frequency and perceptions of cheating; and (3) offered rationales and illustrations to support the idea that cheating is not a healthy thing for students, teachers, or the educational systems and societies in which they function. If those three elements have combined to convince you that cheating should not be ignored, then it seems reasonable to consider what a concerned educator or policymaker could do to begin addressing the problem.

The first step is to become familiar with the methods used to cheat. If educators are unaware of some of the many varieties of ways that students can cheat, they will almost certainly fail to recognize cheating when it occurs.

A Taxonomy of Cheating

The term *taxonomy* is certainly a familiar one in education circles. It denotes a classification system for organizing related ideas or objects. A taxonomy is most helpful when there are many items to be classified and may be especially helpful in an area such as cheating where the behavior is indeed blooming.

In a previous book, I suggested a taxonomy for cheating that lumped specific kinds of cheating into three categories (Cizek, 1999). Those categories of cheating are the following:

- Giving, taking, or receiving information from other persons contrary to the guidelines for the assignment or test. The most common forms of this category include one student whispering an answer to a classmate during a test and two students collaborating on a take-home assignment that was supposed to be completed independently.

- Using any prohibited materials to complete an assignment or test. The most familiar example of this category is the ubiquitous "cheat sheet."

- Capitalizing on the weaknesses of persons, procedures, or processes to gain an advantage on an assignment or test. A rather egregious example of this form of academic dishonesty is when a student gains access to a teacher's grade book left unattended and simply alters his or her grade on an assignment or test.

At the time I developed the three categories, I was considering primarily cheating on tests. However, the categories also seem appropriate for classifying the other major cheating concern—plagiarism. My guess would be that most educators who are concerned about academic dishonesty would attest that cheating on tests and plagiarism on written assignments are the two kinds of cheating that are most commonly encountered. The following sections of this chapter are organized around those two concerns.

Copying, Confederates, Crib Notes, and Collusion

There is nearly an infinite variety of methods that students have used to cheat on tests. The previously mentioned taxonomy is helpful for organizing all of the varieties of cheating, though the taxonomy has its own weaknesses. For one, the taxonomy could benefit from finer subdivisions. For example, the use of prohibited materials could be accomplished via paper copy, electronic, bodily inscription, and so on. Another weakness is that some methods of cheating cannot be easily classified under a single heading as they involve elements of all three domains. For example, one method involves leaving a notebook, textbook, or even a willing and knowledgeable student in a restroom. At an appropriate time during an examination, a test-taker asks to be excused to use the restroom—a request that few teachers would deny.

On arriving at the restroom, the student then reviews his or her notes, reads relevant portions of the textbook, or discusses the question with the knowledgeable accomplice. This method could involve all three domains: the use of forbidden materials, receiving information from other students, and taking advantage of the teacher's good-faith release of the student to use the restroom.

I hasten to mention that the following listing of methods under the various headings of the taxonomy is not exhaustive, but meant only to be indicative of the diversity of methods that are likely to be encountered. All of the methods are ones that I or other researchers have observed, or that students have indicated that they have actually used.

Despite these weaknesses, the classification system should still provide the interested reader with a good introduction to the plethora of possibilities. Finally, as an aside, I assume that many readers of this book will have encountered cheating methods not mentioned here or particularly creative or difficult-to-detect methods. My interest in compiling a taxonomy that is as complete as possible continues, and I encourage such readers to contact me with their anecdotes and any methods I have overlooked. In the following sections, cheating methods within each of the three major domains are presented.

Giving, Taking, or Receiving Information

Some ways that students obtain or exchange information when the directions for the assignment or test prohibit such an exchange include the following:

1. One student looks at another student's test paper, answer sheet, or work, during a test or independent assignment. Usually this is done by simply looking directly at the source material while the student feigns deep contemplation, stretching, or disinterest. However, it can also be done using an aid, such as a small mirror in a compact or makeup case. The mirror is used for the ostensible purpose of inspecting an eyelash, adjusting a contact lens, and so on, but also provides an aid for viewing the paper of a person located nearby.

2. A student may also view the work of another student while purporting to engage the teacher in a conversation about, for example, an unclear test question. During the conversation, the student views the work of students who have already turned in their work on the teacher's desk.

3. One student drops his or her paper on the floor, permitting another student to look at it.

4. Two or more students drop their papers on the floor and pick up a paper that is not their own in order to gain information from a classmate's paper. Repeating the procedure gets the paper back to its owner.

5. Two or more students communicate with sign language, such as hand signals, tapping a pencil, clicking a pen, coughing, and so forth— the variations are seemingly endless. For example, one reporter documented the use of different-colored M&Ms to signal answers to multiple-choice questions (DePalma, 1992). One of my own former students told me about a method in which one student simply tipped her head slightly to the left or right to indicate answers to True/False questions on a test. Other such methods include placing an eraser or other permitted object in a predetermined corner of a desk to indicate an answer to a multiple-choice item (i.e., upper-left corner is A, upper right corner is B, etc.).

6. Two or more students practice the virtue of sharing—by passing back and forth an eraser, ruler, Kleenex, or other permissible item with answers or information inscribed or stored on it. One common derivative of this encountered in the middle school and upper grades involves the sharing of calculators—with the answers to mathematics problems left showing on the display.

7. One student can give answers to multiple-choice questions to an entire class by using a laser pointer and any predetermined points in a classroom. For example, a code is devised using the four corners of the chalkboard or a bulletin board to represent A, B, C, and D. A student can easily signal answers with a laser pointer, which looks like an ordinary pen and projects a beam that would be invisible to a teacher at his or her desk facing the class. A former student told me of a situation in which entire words were spelled out using the letters that appeared on a poster behind the desk (and view) of the teacher.

8. A student can receive information during a test from another student outside the classroom. I have been told of situations in which a student outside a classroom holds up information outside the window in a classroom door; another student told me a situation in which a student lying outside on the ground under a classroom window passed information back and forth to a student inside the classroom.

9. A fast-working student can complete a test or assignment quickly, then write answers on a separate piece of paper or other material. The fast-working student then passes the information to one or more other students when turning in his or her own work, or by depositing the material in a trash can or dropping it on the floor for retrieval by another student.

10. One student takes two copies of a test, two answer sheets, or simply uses a blank sheet of paper in conjunction with a test or assignment that has been distributed by the teacher. The two pieces of paper are placed on top of each other, and the student completes his or her work, taking care to press firmly when writing words, numbers, letters, or filling in the bubbles. To the naked eye, the second copy of the test, the second bubble sheet, or the sheet of paper is innocuous, even if the student happens to be detected passing it to a classmate. However, firm pressure is used to imprint information and the apparently blank document can be passed to a classmate who can read the imprinted answers by holding the paper at an angle to light, feeling the impressions with the fingers, or revealing the information by lightly rubbing over the impressions with pencil lead.

11. Technology has increasingly enabled cheating. Many calculators, personal digital assistants (e.g., Palm Pilots), and other devices permit the exchange of vast amounts of information (not just numbers or equations, but entire text files) via infrared transmission. Many students also carry pagers. A student outside the classroom can simply call in a text or numeric message to another student even during a test. A recent newspaper article dubbed pagers the new "electronic **crib sheet.**"

Using Prohibited Materials

Teachers often decide for themselves which materials students should be prohibited from consulting when they are given an assignment or test. There are probably many situations in which a teacher would not want to preclude students from gaining access to *any* relevant materials, particularly in the context of a longer, independent, or more integrative term project. Teachers vary, too, in their prohibitions in specific contexts. For example, some composition teachers might wish for their students to have access to a dictionary during a writing assignment, others may not; some chemistry teachers may want their students to be able to refer to the periodic table of the elements during a test, others may not. Nothing in this portion of this chapter is intended to impinge on professional judgment or to suggest that such decisions should uniformly be made favoring one approach or another. In the graduate statistics and testing courses that I teach, I use different approaches even within a single examination. For example, I typically require that students memorize the formula that they will have to use to conduct a t test (in fact, I require them to memorize many formulas and to know *which one* should be used to conduct the t test). However, at the same time, I ordinarily permit them to use the tables provided in the back of their textbooks to look up the critical values that will tell them whether the result of the t test they conducted was statistically significant.

That said, it is simply a matter of fact that sometimes teachers judge it appropriate or necessary to prohibit students from accessing information from various sources when they take a test or complete an assignment. A teacher might require students to commit certain formulas to memory or to know key facts, dates, or procedures by rote. There are surely many such situations, and they are clearly not limited to "lower-order" contexts. For example, I suspect that if I needed to visit my physician for an annual physical, my confidence and trust would be shaken if he needed to look up how to perform a blood test and how to interpret the results every year. It is reasonable that, in many situations, teachers may want to ensure that students have mastered "higher-order" processes without relying on their books, notes, and so on. I suspect that even truly "authentic" assessment requires a blended approach: In real life, our students will encounter some situations in which they have access to resources so that they will not need to memorize everything; other situations will require them only to know where to find something quickly; still other situations will require them to complete a product or performance without any aids.

Thus, it is entirely reasonable that, when judged by the teacher to be appropriate for the context, the directions for an assignment or test would prohibit students from using specified materials or resources. In fact, it is probably *only* under such constraints that a teacher can obtain the clearest understanding of a student's independent knowledge or skill. Some of the ways that students obtain access to prohibited materials include the following:

1. Writing information on a piece of paper (a.k.a. "crib sheet") and hiding the paper in any number of locations, such as

- Under the brim of a baseball cap
- On a watchband
- In the barrel of a clear plastic ballpoint pen
- In a watch face
- In a bag of snack food
- In clothing (between pleats, behind a necktie, on a shirttail, etc.)
- In a restroom
- Under a desk or chair

As we saw earlier, a notebook, book cover, or apparently blank paper could actually be a cheat sheet if it had been previously inscribed with information using, for example, a ballpoint pen that has run out of ink such that the inscribed information is visible only when viewed from the correct angle. Relatedly, information can also be printed on a blank sheet of paper using "Wite Out" or "written" onto a desk surface or other surface using an eraser.

2. Writing or carving information in other locations, such as

- On the skin of the forearm, leg, palm, or between the fingers
- On tape or bandages applied to the skin
- On the student's desk or chair surface (or better, on a the back of the chair or side of the desk of a nearby student)
- On the back of a water bottle label
- In the instruction manual for a calculator
- In a textbook, dictionary, or other permitted resource
- In a "spare" blue book
- Into the side of a pencil or eraser
- On a map, poster, or other classroom object
- On a candy or gum wrapper
- On a stick of gum
- On a Kleenex

Of the places where information can be written in the preceding list, the stick of gum and Kleenex warrant special mention as they can be used very cleverly to avoid any trace of the mischief. A fairly large amount of information can be written on a small portion of a Kleenex. A student rarely raises any concern by taking out Kleenex; it becomes in effect a cheat sheet in plain sight. Should a teacher become suspicious, sneezing, coughing, or blowing the nose into the Kleenex is usually sufficient to deter the teacher from pursuing the evidence any further. Using a stick of gum is perhaps the most foolproof method in this domain. A student can write or etch a modest amount of information onto the stick of gum and rewrap it prior to a test. During the test, the piece of gum is unwrapped, the information is accessed, and the gum is chewed, destroying any evidence.

3. Using technological assistance to store or transmit information, such as

- Via a pager or personal digital assistant (e.g., Palm Pilot)
- Using a calculator with the capability of transmission
- Recording spoken information on a cassette tape, burning any kind of information onto a CD-R, or creating .mp3 files and listening to the recordings via a Walkman or personal .mp3 player

These last methods mentioned in the preceding list are particularly powerful because a student can record vast quantities of information onto a CD-R or in .mp3 or .wav format. During an examination or assignment, the student can appear to be listening to music through headphones or, with very small devices such as personal .mp3 players and "ear-buds," it may not even be discernable that the student is listening to anything at all. In fact, if the device is set to continuously repeat, the student may be listening to his or her entire set of course notes, key formulas, important points for an essay, and so on throughout the entire class period.

Taking Advantage of Persons and Processes

The range of possibilities for taking advantage of persons or processes is wide. The range includes behaviors that might be thought of as simply mischievous, while others would actually qualify for criminal prosecution. Illustrations of this range (from, roughly, least to most serious) would include the following:

1. *Happy to Help.* Knowing that most teachers are eager to clarify or assist students during a test or assignment, a student purposefully sits the farthest distance away from where the teacher is seated on the day of a test. At one or more times during the test, the student thinks of (any) question to ask, then takes a long, slow walk to the teacher's seat, viewing the work of other students all along the way.

2. *True or False?* Students can play on a teacher's sense of fair play and the subjectivity of perceptions by writing answers that are purposefully ambiguous. One simple example is shown in Figure 3.1. The figure shows a student's answers to true-false test questions. When in doubt about whether the answer is true or false, the student's answer is written in such a way as to force the teacher to seem unreasonable for disallowing a student to "change" his or her answer.

3. *Oops, My Bad.* Another play on the teacher's sense of fairness occurs when a student changes an answer on a test or assignment after it is graded and returned. There are few ways for a teacher to know for sure that he or she awarded points correctly, mismarked an answer as incorrect, and so forth, so when confronted with an "error" in scoring, many teachers will award the higher score.

4. *Oops, Your Bad.* Another, different kind of play on the teacher's sense of fairness occurs when a student deliberately fails to turn in a test. When the teacher returns graded papers to the class, the student

True/False Test

Directions: Write T on the line provided if the statement is true. Write F on the line if the statement is false.

___F___ 1. All of the countries in central Europe are democracies.

___T___ 2. Great Britain is an example of a monarchy.

___T___ 3. Spain is the only western European country that has a king.

___T___ 4. In a socialist country, most economic decisions are the result of central planning and decision making.

___F___ 5. The European Union (EU) is the name given to a labor union recently formed to benefit people in European countries who work in manufacturing or other industrial labor positions.

Figure 3.1   Taking Advantage of Teacher Subjectivity in Scoring

complains that the teacher must have lost the paper. In many cases, an overworked teacher assumes responsibility for the loss and administers the affected student the same test. If the student did not turn in the test when it was administered, the student will have had ample time to prepare his or her answers for the exact questions on the test.

5. Eenie, Meenie, Miney, Mo. A strategy that can force a teacher to make an uncomfortable choice can be invoked when the teacher prepares a test booklet and a separate answer sheet. If a student is able to narrow down to two the possible correct responses to a multiple-choice question, he or she can write down one of the possible choices in the answer booklet and the other on the answer sheet. If the teacher marks the one answer incorrect, the student can claim that he or she mistranscribed the answer and appeal for the "benefit of the doubt."

6. You Scratch My Back and . . . Peer grading of written assignments and tests is common in many classrooms and was actually the subject of a recent U.S. Supreme Court decision (for a fascinating perspective, see *Owasso Independent School District No. I-011 v. Falvo, 2002*). Peer grading occurs when students exchange papers after completing the test or assignment, and the teacher announces the correct answers. Unfortunately, cheating also occurs. Prior to grading a peer's paper, students make agreements and bargains with each other to award higher scores, overlook incorrect answers, and so on. As in other instances, teachers rarely have the time to monitor peer grading to ensure that the process has not been corrupted by cheating.

7. The Switch-a-Roo. Many teachers require students to provide their own paper or blue books for essay examinations. Because few teachers check to ensure that the paper or blue book is blank before a test, either one of these can be complete with a previously written essay or simply inscribed with helpful information and used during the test.

8. "I Don't Feel Well." Few teachers have the time to construct alternate forms of a test or assignment. Knowing this, a student may be "sick" or otherwise absent from class on the day of a test or may even ask ahead of time to arrange to take the test at an alternate (later) day or time. At minimum, this gives the student additional time to prepare for the test; at worst, the student is able to obtain the exact questions and prepare exemplary answers ahead of time.

9. Testing, One, Two, Three . . . Two opportunities for cheating arise when even conscientious teachers do not keep meticulous track of test materials. For example, when distributing a test or assignment to a class, teachers often simply hand a large number of tests or other materials to the first student in a row, or to several students who are asked to take one copy and pass the pile of remaining copies along to other students. If the teacher has not numbered the materials, or if the teacher has not matched the number of test booklets or the like to the exact number of students in class that day, a student can take an extra set of materials. The extra set can be used by students in other sections who will take the test later. Or the student may not turn in anything at all during the class period. Instead, the student can take the blank test to study hall or another location, fill it in with exemplary responses using prohibited resources, and then leave the test on the floor of the classroom, in a pile near the teacher's desk, and so on. Most teachers would assume that the completed test had simply been misplaced.

Even the rare teacher who develops two forms of a test or assignment may not meticulously track which students were assigned which forms. Thus, for example, a student who obtained prior access to one of the forms could prepare advance responses for that form. If, however, the student was administered a form different from his or her advance copy, the student could indicate that he was responding to "Form A" on his answer sheet as the form he was given.

10. "It's a Substitute, Teacher." In large college classes, a fairly common way of cheating is to take advantage of the fact that the instructor does not know all of the students by name or face. Rather than sit for a test himself, a student can ask a more knowledgeable peer to take the test for him. This kind of cheating is also witnessed on large-scale or high-stakes testing such as the SAT for college admission, and licensure and certification tests for business, professions, and so on. The substitute person who takes the test is sometimes referred to as a "confederate." At the precollegiate level most teachers know their students well enough, and the use of a confederate is not likely to be successful. However, the method can still be used in specific situations, such as when a test is given on a day when there is a substitute teacher who would not be familiar with the class, or when a teacher sends a student to the library or other location to take a makeup test.

11. Grade Change. One of the most direct ways of cheating on any assignment is for a student simply to change a grade that has been recorded in a teacher's grade book when it has been left unattended or in an accessible location. This may actually be one of the most prevalent but underdetected methods of cheating. In one recent case, a high school in Brea Linda, California, was prompted by several incidents of this sort of cheating to conduct an investigation. According to a publicized report, "an independent auditor found over 600 changed grades and other discrepancies in the transcripts of 287 students" (Levine, 1995, p. 68).

12. Gone in 60 Seconds. Most teachers are also remarkably trusting and honest themselves and they assume that their students are as well. Taking advantage of this, students can get an advance copy of an upcoming assignment or test by taking unattended or unsecured materials from a teacher's desk, cabinet, backpack, or briefcase when the teacher is out of the room, at lunch, or simply not attentive to happenings in other parts of the classroom. Other items, such as electronic "test banks," instructor's manuals, or teacher's editions of textbooks containing master copies of quizzes, are often stolen or copied.

Plagiarism

Plagiarism is perhaps even more difficult to recognize than many of the previously mentioned methods of cheating because of the subjectivity involved in judging the degree of similarity between two pieces of written work, and the subjectivity involved in ascertaining a student's knowledge and intent. However difficult these judgments are, the incidence of plagiarism appears to be great and on the increase.

The rise in plagiarism may be due to many factors. As a type of cheating, it would probably be curious if an increase in plagiarism did *not* accompany the documented increases in other forms of cheating. At the elementary and secondary school level, state mandated assessment programs have increased the frequency, importance, visibility, and stakes associated with writing. Advances in computer technology and the Internet have increased the ease and opportunities to engage in plagiarism. Another factor is a continuing reluctance on the part of educators to broach the topic of plagiarism in the classroom and to help students themselves become familiar with the ethics of composition. Finally, many educators simply lack the resources, time, and interest required to become involved in addressing plagiarism, which likely fosters a perception of tolerance or acceptance on the part of their students.

Among the first steps for those concerned about this form of cheating are generating a clear definition of the concept; understanding the educational implications of plagiarism; and acquiring and discussing with students examples of what constitutes plagiarism and what does not.

Defining Plagiarism

The history of the term *plagiarism* is an interesting one. Thomas Mallon, the author of the most extensive academic work on plagiarism, *Stolen Words*, indicates that the term is related to the word "plagiary," which referred to a person who kidnapped a child or slave (Mallon, 1989, p. 6).

According to another author, plagiarism derives from the Latin word *plagiarius*, which referred to a person who steals slaves (Kolich, 1983, p. 143). Kolich refers to plagiarism as "the worm of reason" (p. 141), and he provides a fascinating glimpse into the evolution of the term into its modern usage. According to Kolich, the modern usage was first invented by a Roman poet named Martial. Martial considered his poetic inventions to be the "servants of his imagination." A contemporary of Martial's, Fidentinus, had apparently been taking Martial's poems and reading them as his own. Martial applied the concept of plagiary to this, as Fidentinus was stealing Martial's servants. Kolich concludes his account of this history with the following:

> Martial mockingly and comically ridicules the weaker poet for trying to enslave those who serve the mind of the master. The joke is on Fidentinus since the poems shall rise like rebellious slaves and demand their freedom; Martial triumphs and Fidentinus is the fool, which is his essential punishment for plagiarism. (Kolich, 1983, p. 143)

As we saw with defining cheating generally, it is important to begin a consideration of plagiarism with a concrete idea of the scope and nature of the term, though deriving a useful, modern definition has proven challenging. Reminiscent of the Supreme Court's attempts to define *obscenity,* it can be equally difficult to specify precisely what constitutes plagiarism. For example, it is interesting to note the irony in one source in which it is observed that "academics are pretty much in agreement that no one outstanding definition of plagiarism exists. However, all agree that it is vital to define it for students" (Pearson, 2002, p. 3). In other words, "We can't really define it, but our students must know what it means."

All is not lost, however, and some satisfactory definitions exist. Various authorities have attempted to define the term; the best attempts are usually those that provide abundant examples and nonexamples of plagiarism. A source from the University of California, Berkeley, that is primarily targeted at a collegiate audience, suggests,

> Plagiarism means submitting work as your own that is someone else's. For example, copying material from a book or other source without acknowledging that the words or ideas are someone else's and not your own is plagiarism. If you copy an author's words exactly, treat the passage as a direct quotation and supply the appropriate citation. If you use someone else's ideas, even if you paraphrase the wording, appropriate credit should be given. You have committed plagiarism if you purchase a term paper or submit a paper as your own that you did not write. (Davis, 2002, p. 1)

In their book *Student Cheating and Plagiarism in the Internet Era,* Lathrop and Foss provide some simple parameters that should provide elementary and secondary school students with working concepts of cheating and plagiarism. They recommend that teachers tell their students,

> If you had any help that you don't want your teacher or parents to know about, you probably cheated. If you didn't think of it and write it all on your own, and you didn't cite (or write down) the sources where you found the ideas or the words, it's probably plagiarism. (2000, p. 6)

A Canadian source provides a more elaborated definition of plagiarism in the context of K-12 education:

> Plagiarism, like cheating, is an act that directly challenges the concept of intellectual honesty. It occurs when a person:

1. hands in someone else's work as their own. This applies to direct presentation of someone else's work, a paraphrase of their work, or even direct inclusion of turns of phrase from someone else's writing. In these instances, the plagiarism is most likely intentional.

2. cites sources improperly. Again, this applies to direct quotations, paraphrased ideas, and even turns of phrase. In these instances, the plagiarism may well be unintentional, but it is still plagiarism nonetheless. (*On Plagiarism*, 2002, p. 1)

The preceding definition is provided on the Web site www.2Learn.ca, sponsored by an organization called the "Because We Care Education Society of Alberta." The organization has as its mission "being proactive about the issues to consider in the safe use of the Internet." Along with the very workable definitions of plagiarism for K-12 contexts just provided, the organization has developed a thoughtful statement on the significance of plagiarism for those in K-12 classroom contexts. That statement is reproduced in Figure 3.2.

Plagiarism Methods

Unlike cheating on tests with a nearly infinite variety of methods, plagiarism is accomplished essentially via a single method: taking words or ideas and representing them as one's own or without using appropriate techniques that would indicate the words or ideas are from other sources. "Appropriate techniques" would refer to quotation marks, citations, footnotes, or specific wording acknowledging the source, depending on the specific situation.

The most common ways plagiarism occurs are (1) when a student copies a source verbatim and submits the work as his or her own, and (2) when a student relies on material from a source but makes superficial or other changes to the material so that the submitted work it is not a verbatim copy of the source though it remains essentially an unattributed intellectual effort of another person.

The Whole Enchilada

The first kind of plagiarism—turning in a complete work from another source—is probably not as common as the second kind, because it is the easiest to detect. However, it is also the easiest kind of plagiarism in terms of the student effort required to engage in it, and the teacher effort required to detect it.

- Through intellectual honesty, appropriately recognizing and crediting each other's ideas, we not only substantiate each other's work, but together provide a stronger basis for the development of future ideas.

- Plagiarism, whether intentional or not, directly works against principles of intellectual honesty.

- We must actively foster intellectual honesty among our students if they are to become caring, creative, self-reliant and contributing members of a knowledge-based and prosperous society.

- Intellectual honesty is at the core of advancement in academic scholarship at post-secondary and professional levels. For this reason, plagiarism at the post-secondary level is not tolerated and is subject to severe penalties.

- Educators at the K-12 level must create environments for learning within their classrooms that openly promote and support the culture of life-long intellectual honesty. If plagiarism or cheating occurs at any time, consequences can include a course of action that will not only discourage future infractions but also educate and support the student in engaging in more appropriate behavior in the future.

- Although meeting intentional (or even non-intentional) plagiarism head-on with punitive measures drives home the point that intellectual dishonesty is not to be tolerated within our culture, this might not address the larger issue of how students can learn to share their ideas with pride and with confidence, with the understanding that mutual knowledge construction is a good thing.

- To promote intellectual honesty in K-12 classes is to promote courses of action consistent with the larger ethical values that drive our evolving society.

From "On Plagiarism," http://www.2learn.ca/mapset/SafetyNet/plagiarism/plagiarismframes.html

---

Figure 3.2   Implications of Plagiarism in Elementary and Secondary School Contexts

Although copying an entire work and turning it in as one's own work is the most blatant form of plagiarism, copying intact portions of a work without attribution is also plagiarism. Figure 3.3 provides an example of plagiarism taken from a college handbook in which quoting directly without proper acknowledgement is illustrated. According to the handbook:

Source

For decades, student athletes, usually seventeen- to nineteen-year-old freshmen, have informally agreed to contract with the university to attend athletic performance in exchange for an education. The athletes have kept their part of the bargain; the universities have not. Universities and athletic departments have gained huge gate receipts, television revenues, national visibility, donors to university programs, and more, as a result of the performances of gifted basketball and football players, of whom a disproportionate number of the most gifted and most exploited have been black.

From the Student's Paper

For years, young student athletes have virtually signed four years of their lives away to compete for a university in exchange for a college degree. The athletes have kept their part of the bargain; the universities have not. Universities and athletic departments have gained huge gate receipts, television revenues, national visibility, donors to university programs, and more, as a result of the performances of gifted basketball and football players, of whom a disproportionate number of the most gifted and most exploited have been black.

Figure 3.3   Plagiarism Involving Direct Copying of Source Material

Notes: Source is the work of Harry Edwards, "Educating Black Athletes," *The Atlantic Monthly*, August 1983. Italics indicate plagiarized material. This example is from the University of North Carolina at Chapel Hill, *Graduate School Handbook, 2000-2001*, Chapel Hill, NC: Author.

In this example, the student made changes to the first part of the sentence, then copied directly from the source. All material borrowed from another source must be placed in quotation marks. Quoted material longer than three sentences should be indented without quotation marks. (University of North Carolina at Chapel Hill, 2000, p. 5.30)

This first kind of plagiarism is facilitated increasingly by the availability of electronic resources and the ability to cut and paste material from those sources. Students can exchange answers and ideas via Instant Messenger or e-mail. They can exchange entire assignments or other documents via e-mail. They are very likely to be able to access an electronic encyclopedia that came preinstalled on their home PC.

Most notoriously, students are also able to access an abundance of prepared materials such as entire term papers via the Internet.

According to one writer who has examined the issue, "there are so many easily reached term-paper sites that any student who has access to the Web can get a full-text paper on almost any topic in minutes, and often for free" (O'Leary, 1999, p. 14). In addition to being able to select papers on thousands of topics, students can also select papers written at different levels, and in different languages. Some sites supply downloaded papers at no cost to the student; other sites charge a fee (Visa or MasterCard accepted); still other sites are barter-based—that is, students can get a paper to download for free if they agree to upload a paper on another topic to share with other students. Resource A supplied at the end of this book contains a brief list of some common Internet sites and a basic description of the services and products they provide.

One reason that this kind of plagiarism is not very common is that astute teachers are often easily able to recognize student papers, projects, or other assignments that come from these sources. Teachers usually recognize common text or documents that students have exchanged in the course of reading through a stack of student papers when grading the assignments. And it takes only a few exposures before a teacher is familiar enough with the basic style of Microsoft Encarta, its specific entries on the Civil War, or the essay on the causes of the Revolutionary War downloaded from www.SchoolSucks.com. More difficult to detect—and thus increasingly more common—is the second kind of plagiarism.

Cosmetology 101

The second kind of plagiarism also involves inappropriate appropriation of material, but in this case the student expends some effort to make cosmetic or other changes to the material so that it has a surface appearance or other characteristics that make it less identical to the source.

Figure 3.4 shows another example from the University of North Carolina [UNC] *Handbook.* In addition to providing examples of the kinds of writing that represent infractions of the UNC code of academic integrity, the following passage provides a good example of the kind of direct instruction that can help students avoid plagiarism. According to the *Handbook,*

> In [these passages], the student has recorded the source by substituting words and changing sentences, but keeps the ideas and thoughts of the source. Although the student has reworded the sentences or passage extensively, the author still must be

Source

For decades, student athletes, usually seventeen- to nineteen-year-old freshmen, have informally agreed to contract with the university to attend athletic performance in exchange for an education. The athletes have kept their part of the bargain; the universities have not. Universities and athletic departments have gained huge gate receipts, television revenues, national visibility, donors to university programs, and more, as a result of the performances of gifted basketball and football players, of whom a disproportionate number of the most gifted and most exploited have been black.

From the Student's Paper

Generations of athletes entering colleges and universities across the country have signed a contract with the university to compete in sports, giving their athletic service in exchange for room, board, and tuition.

The athletes have kept their part of the bargain by dedicating themselves to the university for four years; the universities have not, with eight out of ten leaving the university without a college degree. *The sports programs at these universities have profited tremendously from the talent of football and basketball players, of whom, blacks tend to be overrepresented. The dramatic increase in the proportion of black college athletes has paralleled college sports ability to attract television revenues, huge gate receipts, and national viability.*

Figure 3.4   Plagiarism Involving Surface Changes to Source Material

Notes: Source is the work of Harry Edwards, "Educating Black Athletes," *The Atlantic Monthly*, August 1983. Italics indicate plagiarized material. This example is from the University of North Carolina at Chapel Hill, *Graduate School Handbook, 2000-2001*, Chapel Hill, NC: Author.

acknowledged. When used properly, paraphrasing can be a valuable tool for summarizing the author's ideas into your own thoughts. [However], when paraphrasing, if most of the ideas are coming from the source, you must include an appropriate citation to the original author. Paraphrasing, without citation, is plagiarism. (University of North Carolina at Chapel Hill, 2000, p. 5.31)

Another set of examples showing original source, student work, and comment is shown in Figure 3.5. These examples are drawn from Davis (2002). In addition to helping us to gain a clearer idea of what constitutes plagiarism, these samples also provide excellent illustrations of the kinds of examples that are extremely useful for helping students as they learn appropriate writing, research, and citation skills.

Source:

The joker in the European pack was Italy. For a time hopes were entertained of her as a force against Germany, but these disappeared under Mussolini. In 1935 Italy made a belated attempt to participate in the scramble for Africa by invading Ethiopia. It was clearly a breach of the covenant of the League of Nations for one of its members to attack another. France and Great Britain, as great powers, Mediterranean powers, and African colonial powers, were bound to take the lead against Italy at the league. But they did so feebly and half-heartedly because they did not want to alienate a possible ally against Germany. The result was the worst possible: the league failed to check aggression, Ethiopia lost her independence, and Italy was alienated after all.

Plagiarism Example 1

Italy, one might say, was the joker in the European deck. When she invaded Ethiopia, it was clearly a breach of the covenant of the League of Nations; yet the efforts of England and France to take the lead against her were feeble and half-hearted. It appears that those great powers had no wish to alienate a possible ally against Hitler's rearmed Germany.

Comment

This example shows definite plagiarism. Though the facts cited are public knowledge, the stolen phrases aren't. Note that the writer's interweaving of his own words with the source's does not render him innocent of plagiarism.

Plagiarism Example 2

Italy was the joker in the European deck. Under Mussolini in 1935, she made a belated attempt to participate in the scramble for Africa by invading Ethiopia. As J. M. Roberts points out, this violated the covenant of the League of Nations. (J. M. Roberts, History of the World (New York: Knopf, 1976, p. 845.) But France and Britain, not wanting to alienate a possible ally against Germany, put up only feeble and half-hearted opposition to the Ethiopian adventure. The outcome, as Roberts observes, was "the worst possible: the league failed to check aggression, Ethiopia lost her independence, and Italy was alienated after all." (Roberts, p. 845.)

Figure 3.5   Examples Showing Degrees of Plagiarism and Acceptable Paraphrasing

Notes: Source material is from Roberts, J. M. (1976). *History of the World*. New York: Knopf, p. 845. Plagiarism examples, non-example, and comments are taken from Davis (2002).

(Continued)

Figure 3.5 (Continued)

Comment

Still plagiarism. The two correct citations of Roberts serve as a kind of alibi for the appropriating of other, unacknowledged phrases. But the alibi has no force: Some of Roberts' words are again being presented as the writer's.

Non-plagiarism Example 1

Much has been written about German rearmament and militarism in the period 1933-1939. But Germany's dominance in Europe was by no means a foregone conclusion. The fact is that the balance of power might have been tipped against Hitler if one or two things had turned out differently.

Take Italy's gravitation toward an alliance with Germany, for example. That alliance seemed so very far from inevitable that Britain and France actually muted their criticism of the Ethiopian invasion in the hope of remaining friends with Italy. They opposed the Italians in the League of Nations, as J. M. Roberts observes, "feebly and half-heartedly because they did not want to alienate a possible ally against Germany." (J. M. Roberts, History of the World, New York: Knopf, 1976, p. 845.) Suppose Italy, France, and Britain had retained a certain common interest. Would Hitler have been able to get away with his remarkable bluffing and bullying in the later thirties?

Comment

No plagiarism. The writer has been influenced by the public facts mentioned by Roberts, but he hasn't tried to pass off Roberts' conclusions as his own.

Word processors make the second kind of plagiarism very easy to accomplish. Using the "search and replace" function allows students to edit references in the body of the paper. For example, suppose a teacher at Aurora High School assigns her students the task of writing a persuasive essay in which the students are asked to take a position on whether Aurora High should allow students to come and go at will from school grounds during the school day. A student who finds an Internet paper titled "Why We Should Have an Open-Campus Policy at Evergreen High School" can easily search and replace "Evergreen" with "Aurora" and, in nanoseconds, have a custom-tailored persuasive essay.

Nearly all word processors also have spell checkers, thesauruses, and grammar checkers. A quick run of the spell checker can assist the student in ensuring that any telltale misspellings are corrected. Running a thesaurus utility permits students to replace simple word choices with more sophisticated ones (or vice versa). Grammar checking utilities often even suggest alternate wordings for entire phrases or sentences. In summary, just a few minutes of effort using the options available on nearly every student's computer can transform an essay obtained from another source into a product that bears little surface resemblance to the original.

Conducting composition cosmetology is a strategy used by students for their own work, but it is also apparently an entrepreneurial activity. According to one high school junior,

> I got this computer and it came with an encyclopedia. . . . Somebody comes up to me and says, "I need ten pages on Edgar Allen Poe." I can go home, cut and paste, and depending on how smart the person is, I'll add what is appropriate. (quoted in McCabe, 1999, p. 683)

Conclusions and a Caution

Several conclusions about how cheating occurs are clear. Cheating is fairly easy to do. If a student wants to do so, there is a nearly infinite variety of methods that can be used to cheat on a test or project, or to plagiarize for a term paper or written assignment. Students are remarkable for their ability to invent new strategies for short-circuiting assessments of their learning and for shortening the time they would be required to spend on assignments. Student ingenuity has been supplemented by technological advances that make cheating even easier. Combined with what we learned in the previous chapter about the increasing frequency of cheating and its cost to students, educational systems, and society, there is good reason to be concerned.

All of these things notwithstanding, it is also important for educators to be aware of other important facts and to exercise some caution regarding suspicions of cheating by students. First, though the data show that cheating is easy and a majority of students admit to doing it at one time or another, under reasonable conditions most students *do not cheat* on most tests and assignments. (We go into detail about what conditions a teacher might implement in Chapter 5.)

Second, although there is clearly a rationale for why teachers should know about the many kinds of cheating so that they can be alert for them, there is a concomitant risk that such knowledge can make us too cynical. We must work to avoid the tendencies to suspect all students of cheating, to see plagiarism in every student term paper, to be overly wary of every baseball cap, and to create classroom climates in which students are assessed in military-style arrangements attended by suspicious proctors who interpret any pupil's stray eye movement as a nefarious subversion.

Some of the most important but fragile relationships are those created between students and their teachers. To foster student learning, risk taking, creativity, trust, and respect for others, the classroom environment must be one in which cheating is defined, identified, and condemned. To this end, we examine methods that teachers can use to detect cheating in the next chapter. However, it is equally important that concerns about cheating are not intrusive, and that those concerns and a knowledge of methods used to cheat foster a healthy awareness—not an atmosphere of anxiety, suspicion, or mistrust.

Questions for Further Discussion

What kinds of cheating have you observed or heard about that . . .

> Are not among those listed in this chapter?

> Are particularly hard or easy to detect?

Some people might say, "If students just put as much energy and creativity into their schoolwork as they do into cheating, they wouldn't need to cheat." Do you agree or disagree with that statement? Why or why not?

CHAPTER 4

How Can Cheating Be Detected and Addressed?

Awareness of the methods used to cheat on tests or quizzes and to plagiarize work for a term paper or written assignment is a first step toward being able to detect cheating. In addition, however, there are specific things that teachers can do to identify instances of possible cheating. The sections of this chapter provide some concrete ideas—some traditional, some involving the use of technology—for detecting cheating in a variety of situations. The chapter concludes with a few tips for responding to cheating if it is suspected. First, however, I examine the role of inference in detecting cheating.

An Introduction to Inference

I have spoken with some teachers who claim that they have a pretty good idea if a student is cheating just by observing his or her behavior during a test: "If a student avoids eye contact with me [the teacher], seems nervous or fidgety, or if I see them exchanging glances with another student, there's a good chance that they're cheating."

I suppose that experienced teachers often have reason to believe that a student is cheating. However, it is important to realize that student behaviors such as those mentioned are just as easily interpretable as embarrassment, test anxiety, and so on. In these cases, the student's behavior is called *high inference*—which means that it is necessary to make a long leap from what is observed to the actual motivation of the student or the real meaning of the behavior. On the other hand, it is safest to rely on *low inference* behavior or more clear-cut evidence.

Suppose that a teacher observes a student who is using a Palm Pilot during a history test, contrary to the directions that the teacher gave. The teacher who gives the student a failing grade for the test because "she cheated" has made the strong inference that the student used the digital assistant to look up or exchange information. But perhaps the student was only checking whether she had volleyball practice that night. Perhaps she was writing a note to herself to return a book to the library. Maybe she was looking up the correct spelling of a word.

Are these things cheating? Strictly speaking, if the teacher forbade the use of items such as Palm Pilots, then the student has broken the rules. However, the teacher would have to infer what the student was actually doing with the Palm Pilot in order to conclude that cheating had occurred. If the student were truly doing one of the fairly innocuous things mentioned previously, then the teacher would be incorrectly concluding the student had cheated. And if the purpose of the history test was to measure students' knowledge of the Reconstruction, then assigning a failing grade to the student for "cheating" would result in a seriously distorted—that is, an *invalid*—idea about the student's true knowledge or skill on that topic.

On the other hand, suppose that the teacher was able to confiscate the student's Palm Pilot and found that two of the chapters of the textbook had been downloaded onto it. The inference that the student had cheated would be stronger, but still not clear-cut. For example, though the student *could* have had the material available, the teacher would still be having to infer that the student was accessing the material when she was using the Palm Pilot. It is still plausible that the student was not accessing the material; perhaps she had downloaded the material onto the Palm Pilot several weeks ago and had used it to read and study from prior to the test. Thus it still requires a moderate inference about the student's behavior to conclude that the student was cheating.

Finally, let's suppose all of the following:

- The teacher was able to confiscate the student's Palm Pilot
- The Palm Pilot contained two chapters of the textbook that had been downloaded onto it
- The chapters were those covered by the current test
- The student's essay on the Reconstruction contained some entire sentences that were taken verbatim from the chapters

It would seem like an open-and-shut case. The extent of inference required to conclude that the student cheated has reduced dramatically. But has the need to infer that the student has cheated disappeared altogether? No. Clearly there are reasonable explanations that the student could offer to for the verbatim sentences. Perhaps she and a classmate memorized several such sentences containing key facts about the Reconstruction, knowing that such information would be helpful on the test.

In fact, one of the most difficult cheating cases I have ever dealt with in my own teaching involved three students who gave identical answers to all 60 items on a multiple-choice final examination. They got *exactly* the same questions right, they got *exactly* the same questions wrong, and for the questions they got wrong, they even chose *exactly the same wrong answer in every case.* Surely this was a clear-cut case of cheating, I thought, and I had plenty of additional information that strengthened that inference. I noticed their suspicious behavior during the test, the fact that the three were good friends, their abysmal performance on the midterm examination and other assignments, their lack of participation in class, and more. I confronted the students about what I inferred to be cheating on the final examination, and I asked them for any plausible explanation to counter the inference of cheating. They explained that they had studied together.

Laughable? Perhaps. But it is also plausible. It is not impossible that students who studied together would get the same questions correct and incorrect. It is also conceivable that they would choose the very same wrong answers if their studying reinforced common misunderstandings.

In the end, much additional evidence was brought to bear in the case I faced, and the students were, in fact, guilty of cheating. However, I tell the story to highlight the notion that, however objective we may believe our observations of cheating to be, they still require inference. In addition to being vigilant about the possibility of cheating, educators have an obligation to be equally vigilant in assessing the extent of inference required to conclude that cheating has occurred and to rule out (or in) plausible alternative explanations. With that caution, we now turn to some practical tips for detecting cheating on tests and plagiarism on written assignments.

Practical Tips for Detecting Cheating on Tests

The foremost piece of advice regarding what teachers can do to detect cheating on tests is also the most commonsensical. A leading college textbook in the area of testing recommends that the teacher should always be in the room and be alert while the test is being given. According to the authors of the book, "The best way to detect cheating is to observe students during the examination—not by being preoccupied at one's desk" (Mehrens & Lehmann, 1991, p. 158). Stated differently, a teacher is not likely to see any cheating if he or she isn't looking. Demonstrating a serious and attentive demeanor during tests is also a key way of preventing cheating.

Low-Tech Methods

There are a number of simple ways that teachers can be on the lookout for factors that are suggestive of cheating. A sampling of these factors is shown in Table 4.1. Of course, as we saw in the previous section, all of the student behaviors listed in the table should be interpreted with caution, and with attention to the extent of inference required.

As many experienced teachers know, students who cheat often have a number of techniques that they use to avoid suspicion. Students may consciously perform actions intended specifically to deflect the teacher's attention—strategies that have actually been investigated by researchers and given a name: "impression management" (Albas & Albas, 1993, p. 451). The researchers found that these behaviors are often used by innocent students to ensure that they are not suspected of cheating. A list and descriptions of five impression management techniques is shown in Figure 4.1.

High-Tech Methods

Statisticians have invented highly sophisticated techniques for detecting cheating on tests. These statistical procedures have been incorporated into powerful software programs that provide remarkably sensitive and accurate methods for detecting cheating in (primarily) large-scale testing contexts, such as those involving 100 or more students (to be clear, I should add that these software programs are really able to detect only answer copying, not all forms of cheating on tests).

Any in-depth description of either the statistical techniques used or the various software programs is beyond the scope of this book, though I have reviewed them in greater depth elsewhere (see Cizek, 1999). However, at least one of these high-tech tools deserves mention—a software program called *Scrutiny!*—because of its user-friendly nature and potential for use with small groups of test-takers, such as the 25 or so students that might be encountered in a typical classroom.

Table 4.1   Potential Indications of Cheating on Tests

Before a test, a teacher . . .

1. Discovers that there are missing copies of tests or the answer key
2. Observes that one or more students seem unconcerned about the upcoming test
3. Notices that one or more students take seats that differ from the locations where they usually sit
4. Sees information written on desk surfaces, chalkboards, etc.
5. Hears reports from students about potential cheating

During a test, a student . . .

1. Is absent
2. Wears a baseball cap
3. Uses headphones
4. Avoids eye contact with teacher
5. Seems unusually nervous, anxious
6. Frequently drops pen, sharpens pencil, etc.
7. Uses restroom frequently/for an unusually long time
8. Fidgets with materials in desk, book bag, clothing, etc.
9. Exchanges materials with any other student
10. Appears to be looking at another student's test
11. Completes the test in an unexpectedly short period of time

After a test, a teacher . . .

1. Observes that a student's performance is dramatically better than his or her previous work
2. Notices unusual similarities in two or more students' work
3. Notices unusual similarities between a student's work and material in a textbook, etc.
4. Finds pieces of paper with information on the floor, etc.
5. Hears reports that cheating has occurred

Scrutiny! (Advanced Psychometrics Incorporated, 1993) is available from Assessment Systems Corporation (ASC) of St. Paul, Minnesota. The suggested price of *Scrutiny!* ($399.00) is in line with the cost of similar statistical programs. Admittedly, the cost would put the program out of reach for most individual classroom teachers, but it may be reasonable for a school building or district.

The program is available only in a Windows version, but is configured to run on almost any personal computer with a Pentium I or better processor. An easy-to-use and complete demonstration version

1. Staring: when a student keeps his or her eyes fixed on the teacher during a test

According to Albas and Albas, "the theory is that if the [teacher] sees students looking at them, they could not possibly be looking at anybody or anything else" (p. 455).

2. Smiling: when a student shows unusual happiness or affection toward a teacher during a test

According to Albas and Albas, "one young woman reports that she smiles ingenuously at the [teacher] and moves her eyebrows up and down a few times because as she says, 'no cheater would be comfortable enough to do a goofy thing like that'" (p. 455).

3. Mourning: when a student portrays a forlorn, lost, or hopeless expression during a test

According to Albas and Albas, "one young male student indicates: 'I've given the [teachers] a sort of "help me, I'm stuck" look, hoping that it may have made them feel sorry for me and so cancel out any thoughts they may have had that I might be cheating'" (p. 455).

4. Organizing: when a student demonstrates unusual attention to keeping his or her belongings in order, straightening them, etc.

According to Albas and Albas, "under such circumstances the management of these materials [i.e., unauthorized books, notes, formulas] has to be elaborate and intensive in order to convince [teachers] that they are not being used illicitly. One man states that he piles these materials on the floor beside his desk with the ones pertaining to the course and might be of any use at the bottom" (p. 456).

5. Seating: when a student chooses a seat in the classroom typically different from his or her usual seat, and that because of its location would be either difficult for the teacher to observe or so conspicuously in the teacher's view as to not arouse suspicion

Albas and Albas report that "some students sit directly in front of the [teacher] so that they can be ostentatiously innocent" while others "avoid seats beside the well known high achievers because they may be suspected of trying to copy from them. Also avoided are seats next to known cheaters" (p. 457).

Figure 4.1   Five "Impression Management" Techniques

Adapted from Albas & Albas, 1993, pp. 455–457.

of the software can be downloaded quickly from the ASC Web site (www.assess.com). According to the documentation provided with *Scrutiny!*, the program requires the following hardware and companion software to operate successfully:

- A Windows operating system (version 3.1, 95, 98, or later)
- The Windows programs Write, WordPad, Paintbrush, Paint, and Notepad (these are usually installed as part of the Windows operating system)
- Approximately 2 MB of free hard disk space for installation of *Scrutiny!*
- Approximately 5 MB of free hard space for working files
- At least 4 MB of RAM

To run *Scrutiny!*, a teacher is required to prepare a test data input file, though this is done with any common word processing program such as Microsoft Word, WordPerfect, and others. The input file contains the answer key for the test items, and students' answers to the test questions. The input file may also include up to nine information fields (such as for students' names) and students' seat locations.

Scrutiny! then provides several analyses; the most relevant for our purposes here is called the "Suspicious Similarities Report," in which students with patterns of unusually similar incorrect answers are identified. These suspicious pairs are highlighted when the odds that two students produced the same patterns of incorrect answers by random chance are less than 1 in 10,000. One of the most easy-to-interpret pieces of *Scrutiny!* output is a graph showing a distribution of test results, with highly suspect results shown as outliers from the rest of the students' performances. One such graphic, produced from the sample data that accompanies the demonstration version of the program, is reproduced in Figure 4.2. As the figure illustrates, there appears to be one pair of students (the result shown as a short bar on the chart between a similarity value of 6 and 7) for whom the similarity in incorrect responses is not likely due to chance.

Practical Tips for Detecting Plagiarism

There are also practical steps teachers can take to be on guard for plagiarism in student-written assignments. As with cheating on tests, some of these methods are more traditional, low-tech, or routine;

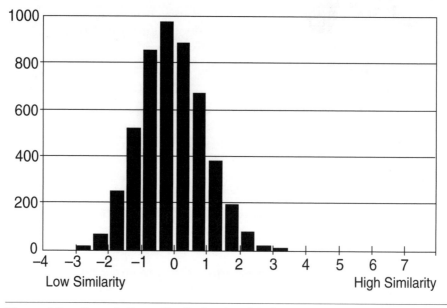

Figure 4.2   Sample Error Similarity Graphic from *Scrutiny!* Cheating
                   Detection Software

others involve the use of technology to investigate potential plagiarism. The following sections provide a sampling of what is available. In
addition to the resources described in detail in the following sections,
a more extensive listing of resources, organizations, books, Web sites,
and software to help educators detect and prevent cheating is provided
in Resource C.

Low-Tech Methods

It is likely that experienced composition teachers perform plagiarism checks almost automatically. If pressed, they could probably list
numerous telltale signs that the work submitted by a student is not his
or her own. A number of authors have attempted to assemble and
organize this tacit wisdom of teachers, and many of these collections
are readily accessible via the Internet. One such collection is shown in
Figure 4.3. This list is drawn from the work of Bates and Fain (2002),
and it provides some examples of the signs that can indicate to a
teacher that a student's writing may not be original.

A student's work may be plagiarized if . . .

1. The writing style, language, vocabulary, tone, grammar, or other features of the composition are not commensurate with what the student usually produces.

2. The "voice" of the writing doesn't sound like the student.

3. There are awkward changes in verb tense, pronouns, structure, or organization of the paper.

4. Sections or sentences in the composition seem out of place or do not relate to the overall content of the paper or to the writing skills and/or content that has been taught. Or, after a relevant introduction, the student's paper changes to become less obviously relevant to the assignment. (According to Bates and Fain, 2002, this occurs when a student "personalizes" a paper obtained from another class or from another source by simply adding material in an attempt to link less relevant material to the specific class assignment.)

5. Strange text, such as a date in the footer of a paper or a URL (Web site address) in a header appears at the top or bottom of printed pages.

6. The work contains changes in font, pitch, color, or shading on the printed page. This can indicate that the work was downloaded from the Internet or cut-and-pasted from another source.

7. There is unusual formatting or page layout, such as line spacing, margin changes, pagination, etc., that doesn't appear homogeneous or correct.

8. The paper contains references to graphs, charts, accompanying material, citations, chapters, footnotes, or additional text that isn't there.

9. The essay mentions ideas, persons, settings, etc., with which the student is not likely to be familiar.

10. The student's work contains citations or references to sources or materials to which the student is not likely to have access.

11. The citations or references list are missing, inaccurate, or incomplete.

12. When asked, the student has difficulty summarizing his or her paper or responding to simple questions about what he or she wrote.

Figure 4.3   Potential Indications of Plagiarism

Adapted from Bates and Fain (2002, p. 1).

High-Tech Methods

Turnabout is fair play. Just as students who intend to plagiarize have found assistance in the availability of electronic resources and the Internet, teachers, too, can take advantage of these tools to help them detect cheating. The two most common ways that plagiarism can be detected via technology include (1) the use of general search engines and (2) the use of databases specifically designed for teachers.

Search Engines

Anyone who uses the Internet is familiar with the dozens of search engines available; that is, with Web sites that are dedicated to cataloging and organizing the vast amounts of information that can be found on the World Wide Web. Some of the more familiar search engines (and their URLs) include:

1. Google (www.google.com)
2. Metacrawler (www.metacrawler.com)
3. Yahoo! (www.yahoo.com)
4. AltaVista (www.altavista.com)
5. Excite (www.excite.com)
6. Dogpile (www.dogpile.com)

To use a search engine, a user would type in one of the Web addresses listed above to go to the Web site of the search engine. In most cases, the site then provides a box into which the user types a word or phrase. The search engine then finds the most relevant Web sites containing the word or phrase and displays them in a summary format. For example, suppose that a person was looking for information to help plan a summer camping trip to a national park. The person could type in the word *vacation* and execute a search. Unfortunately, there are several hundreds of thousands of Web sites around the world that include the term "vacation" and the person would likely be overwhelmed with the results of the search and unable to locate the specific information that he or she was looking for. On the other hand, the same user could type in three terms, such as "vacation," "national parks," and "camping." This would greatly refine the work of the search engine, and the result would be a much smaller, more relevant, and manageable set of results related to the user's specific interest.

None of these general search engines is specifically designed for detecting plagiarism. However, through the adept use of search terms, a teacher can easily adapt them to that task. For example, suppose that a teacher assigned an essay on the topic "Famous Artists of the Renaissance." The teacher suspects that a student's essay may have been cut-and-pasted from an Internet source. Using a search engine, the teacher could attempt to retrieve all Internet sources that addressed the same topic and compare the student's essay to those found on the Internet. The search engine could be used to

• Search for Web pages containing the key terms "art" and "Renaissance." This strategy would not likely be the most effective because of the very large number of results that would be retrieved. However, for very narrow topics or highly unusual terms, this strategy might be sufficient.

• Search for an unusual term or misspelling. For example, suppose that a student includes the alliterative phrase "piquant portraiture" to describe a Renaissance artist's work, or the student consistently misspells the word *"Renaissance"* with the spelling "Renissonce." A teacher could search for either of these oddities to locate Web sites in which the same flair or error appear—sites that would be relatively few in number and potentially the source of plagiarized material.

• Search for a specific bit of writing found in a student's paper. For example, suppose an introductory sentence in the student's essay was, "Many scholars have studied the impact of Renaissance painters on subsequent generations of artists." A teacher can type in this entire sentence in quotation marks and locate any sources that contain the exact same wording. Because the search will return only results that contain this exact sentence, any result is highly likely to be a plagiarized source.

Plagiarism Web Sites

Most Web sites related to plagiarism are dedicated to helping students access term papers or reports. However, a few sites provide online plagiarism detection services for teachers. One such site is sponsored by Glatt Plagiarism Services, Inc. That company's Web site (www.plagiarism.com) provides a wealth of information about plagiarism, and two detection options: (1) a demonstration plagiarism detection program, and (2) a full-version detection program.

The demonstration version is called the "Glatt Plagiarism Self-Detection Program." This program requires that a brief portion of a student's writing be entered into a small, on-screen text box. Then, the user submits the writing sample and, over the Internet, the student's writing sample is returned, but with words omitted in a systematic way. For example, every fifth word is deleted and replaced with a uniformly sized blank. Then, much like the cloze procedures that many reading teachers are familiar with, the student is asked to insert the correct words into the blanks without looking at his or her original essay. When the student is finished filling in the missing words, the portion is resubmitted for scoring, which consists of the percentage of missing words correctly identified.

When used to detect plagiarism, the software operates under the assumption that a student who is the author of a writing sample should be familiar enough with his or her own style and content to correctly fill in a high percentage of the missing words. A student who had plagiarized would not.

The demonstration version of the software operates entirely over the Internet and is found at www.plagiarism.com/self.detect.htm. The same software can be purchased for on-site use (i.e., not Internet-based) if a teacher wishes to have a version installed on a classroom computer. That version is available for Windows 95/98/NT operating systems for $65.

The more sophisticated and accurate version of this product is called the "Glatt Plagiarism Screening Program." Complete ordering information is available at the plagiarism.com Web site mentioned previously. The program costs $300 if purchased individually, or $250 if purchased in conjunction with plagiarism tutorial software also offered by the company.

A highly advanced and powerful alternative to the Glatt site can be found at www.turnitin.com. To use this system, a teacher submits a complete student essay, term paper, or report. Naturally, this requires an electronic version of the document. However, because teachers are increasingly requiring electronic submissions (and even if they don't, their students probably prepared and saved their work electronically), this requirement becomes less of an obstacle every day.

The student's essay is then scrutinized by comparing words, phrases, and sentences with those in documents found all over the World Wide Web as well as in a proprietary database of student work previously submitted to the site. In the end, the teacher receives a custom report for each student essay called an "Originality Report" that includes a summary index expressing the overall degree of similarity between the student's essay and all of the other sources. According to developers of the system, Originality Reports are

> exact duplicates of submitted papers, except that any text either copied or paraphrased from the Internet appears underlined, color-coded, and linked to its original online source. Subscribers receive [Originality Reports] for every submitted assignment . . . usually within 24 hours. . . . Each color-coded passage in the report has a corresponding live link to a source

on the Internet. Clicking on a link opens a new window to that source. Depending on the results, users have the option of adding or excluding Web addresses to their search. (http://www. turnitin.com/services_1.html)

This service is available to teachers in secondary schools at an individual rate of $75 per year. That rate covers six classes, 100 Originality Reports, and only one instructor. Individual teachers can try out the system for free (five free Originality Reports) by registering at www. turnitin.com/free_trial.html.

A different (discounted) price structure is available for schools and school districts, depending on the size of the school or district and the particular type of service configuration selected. Specific cost quotes can be obtained at the site; the estimated cost provided at the site is approximately 50¢ per student per school year.

Plagiarism Software

In addition to general Internet search engines and Internet-based detection systems, a number of stand-alone software programs have been specifically designed to help teachers spot instances of potential plagiarism. The programs are purchased or licensed from their developers and are installed on a local computer for use in the classroom or school.

One example of such software is called EVE version 2.0 (or EVE2); "EVE" stands for "essay verification engine." Information on the software is available at http://www.canexus.com/eve/

According to the developers of EVE2, the program

allows professors and teachers at all levels of the education system to determine if students have plagiarized material from the World Wide Web. EVE2 accepts essays in plain text, Microsoft Word, or Corel Word Perfect format and returns links to web pages from which a student may have plagiarized. . . . EVE2 performs a large number of complex searches to find material from any Internet site. . . . Not only does it find these suspect sites, but it then does a direct comparison of the submitted essay to the text appearing on the suspect site. If it finds evidence of plagiarism, the URL is recorded. Once the search has completed, the teacher is given a full report on each paper that contained plagiarism, including the percent of the essay plagiarized, and an annotated copy of the paper showing all plagiarism highlighted in red. (http://www.canexus.com/ eve/abouteve.shtml)

Teachers interested in trying the EVE2 software can download a copy of EVE and use it without charge for a 15-day trial period. After that, the product can be purchased for $19.99 per licensee (i.e., per teacher). It is worth noting that this is a one-time cost to purchase the product. According to the information at the company's site, anyone who purchases the software is eligible for a free update whenever an upgrade of EVE2 is released. Or, if a new version of the software is developed (e.g., EVE3), those who have purchased EVE2 will be able to purchase the new version at a reduced cost.

Responding to Cheating

When a teacher suspects that a student has cheated on a test or assignment, the teacher faces one of the most difficult challenges of his or her professional life. The response (or lack of response) sets many wheels in motion and can have lasting effects on students, parents, fellow teachers, administrators, and the school environment. In addition, responding to cheating is a skill many teachers lack familiarity with and that was almost certainly not addressed in their preservice training or professional development. Of course, teachers are not alone. Neither they nor their principals were likely trained in how to respond to cheating in a way that is both appropriate and fair to all those involved. As a result, cheating is often simply ignored.

The Problem of Ignoring Cheating

Students increasingly report that their teachers either let them cheat or show no interest in preventing cheating. Consider the following observations of junior high school students who participated in a focus group on cheating:

> Student 1: "Cheating is kind of considered, I don't know, just a kind of daily thing that's out there, almost kind of acceptable. Teachers know it and students know it."
> Student 2: "We haven't actually had many tests this year, but when we do, people just kind of pass around papers and whatever. I think the teacher knows, but he just doesn't do anything about it." (quoted in McCabe, 1999, pp. 682, 685)

These anecdotal reports are borne out in larger-scale research on what students say their teachers think about cheating. In the study by Brandes (1986), 4.3% of elementary school students said that their teachers "do nothing" in response to cheating; by high school, 20.2% of students said that cheating was ignored. More than 15 years later, a similar large-scale study was conducted. This time, 47% of high school students reported that "teachers in their school sometimes ignore cheating" (McCabe, 2001, p. 40). Thus, it would seem that ignoring cheating only helps ensure that the behavior will continue.

Why Responding Is Difficult

Confronting cheating is difficult for many reasons. For one, as we saw previously, a suspicion of cheating almost always involves inference. Cheating is almost never clear-cut. A student is almost never caught red-handed. The evidence is almost always ambiguous.

Another reason that responding to cheating is difficult is that teachers tend to *want* to believe the best about their students. We are considerably more comfortable supporting and advocating for students; we are less comfortable playing the roles of inquisitor, disciplinarian, or snitch. By responding to cheating, we risk a breaking down of the relationships with students and the open classroom environments that we spend much of our time building up.

According to a recent article on plagiarism at the college and university level, the reluctance of teachers to respond to cheating was attributed to a

> preference for handling suspected plagiarism privately between faculty and student, as a counseling matter or not at all. Some faculty feel that they are in the business of teaching specific subject matter, not discipline or moral values. (Schneider, 1999, p. A-8)

At the high school level, one author reports that "schools are reluctant to punish students who cheat because they fear a confrontation with their parents" (Levine, 1995, p. 68).

Finally, responding to cheating can seem like a lose-lose situation. Obviously, a student loses when he or she resorts to cheating in place of actually learning material, preparing the written assignment, conducting the lab experiment, and so on. The student also loses if he or she is caught cheating and is punished with a lower grade, the loss of esteem of his or her peers, or reprimands from parents. Teachers can lose much time responding to cheating, especially if it involves conferences with the student, the principal, the student's parents, and—in very serious situations—with attorneys or others involved in a disciplinary hearing, legal proceeding, or appeal. According to a survey of high school students,

The most frequent explanation [for teachers' ignoring cheating] mentioned by 26 percent of students, was that teachers often don't want to accuse a student of cheating because of the bureaucratic procedures involved in pursuing such allegations. (McCabe, 2002, p. 40)

Teachers also risk losing a friendship with the student and the student's family; teachers often also risk losing professional relationships among their colleagues who do not view cheating in the same way, or who have a personal or political stake in avoiding responding to cheating. School administrators lose the time that they must invest in proceedings related to cheating; they must spend time responding to calls from angry parents; sometimes they must work to address a full-blown crisis.

All in all, there are often more incentives for teachers to ignore cheating than to respond to it. Two case studies illustrate this state of affairs. The first involves a Texas teacher who decided that his response to cheating was not worth the price. The second involves a Kansas teacher who paid a high price for her concern.

In the words of the Texas high school teacher:

In the first grading period, I boldly flunked a number of students, including the daughter of an administrator of a local elementary school and a star fullback who was also the nephew of a school board member. Shortly thereafter I was called in to meet with my principal and the aggrieved parents. Such was my naïveté that I actually bothered to bring evidence. I showed the elementary administrator her daughter's plagiarized book report and the book from which it had been copied, and I showed the fullback's father homework bearing his son's name but written in another person's handwriting. The parents offered weak apologies but maintained that I had not treated their children fairly.

[Afterward] my principal suddenly discovered a number of problems with my teaching. For the next few weeks he was in my class almost daily. Every spitball, every chattering student, every bit of graffiti was noted. When there were discipline problems my superiors sided with the offending students. Teaching became impossible.

So I learned to turn a blind eye to cheating and plagiarism and to give students, especially athletes, extra credit for everything from reading orally in class to remembering to bring their pencils. In this way I gained the cooperation of my students and the respect and support of my superiors. (quoted in Bishop, Mane, Bishop, & Moriarty, 2000, p. 4)

A television station near Kansas City reported the case of the second teacher, who learned a different lesson in January 2002:

> It was the end of the fall semester at Piper High School, 4400 North 107th St. A final project to collect and describe leaves for 10th grade biology. Teacher Christine Pelton noticed a disturbing trend. "They were giving the same report, word-for-word," Pelton says.
>
> Pelton went to the Web and matched up entire paragraphs from some papers, then told the students they'd plagiarized. "The kids claim they didn't know how to cite and what plagiarism was, and we covered it in class," Pelton says. She referred them to the district handbook they received at the beginning of the year and the policy inside. She referred them to the same policy on the syllabus, which the kids and their parents had signed.
>
> Then, based on the policy, she gave 30 students, about a quarter of the class, a zero on the project. The project was worth 50 percent of the semester grade. That's how the teacher before her had done it; that's how she did it. Flunking the project meant flunking the course, so parents complained to the teacher and then the school board.
>
> The board, in turn, revised its own plagiarism policy and applied it to Pelton's class. Then the board revised Pelton's policy about the weight of the grade, from 50 percent to 30. . . .
>
> Pelton says the decision undermined her authority, and made it practically impossible to keep teaching at the school. "When [the students] found out, they started cheering, 'We won. We won. We don't have to listen to you any longer' that 'teachers need to realize that we run the school, not you'" Pelton says.
>
> That's why she resigned a month ago. The school superintendent confirmed all of the facts that Pelton presented to KCTV-5, but did not express an opinion on the board's decision, saying, quote "I don't want to pick at that scab again." (Teacher Resigns, 2002)

Specific Strategies for Responding

In the best of all worlds, teachers would not be confronted with cheating. Indeed, the proverb applies here: An ounce of prevention is worth a pound of cure. And, in the next chapter, we look at some ways to prevent cheating. Nonetheless, a teacher who is familiar with the methods students use to cheat and who is observant will—perhaps

Table 4.2   Points to Remember When Responding to Cheating

1. Take the matter seriously.
2. Be aware of subjectivity and inference.
3. Consider the good of all students.
4. Gather and maintain evidence.
5. Involve other professionals.
6. Maintain confidentiality.
7. Make the punishment fit the crime.

many times over his or her career—be faced with responding to a difficult situation. If a teacher decides to respond to a suspicion of cheating, there are a few important points to remember. These points are described in the following paragraphs and summarized in Table 4.2.

First, take the matter seriously, both beforehand and afterward. I have seen teachers joke with their students, as in, "Bill, do you need to move a little closer to Sarah so that you have a better view of her paper?" One responsibility of the teacher is to promote a serious attitude toward learning and assessment, and to ensure that fairness prevails in a classroom. If a teacher jokes about cheating, it is unlikely that students will take it seriously either.

Second, be aware of your own background with any student you suspect of cheating. Keep in mind that the frustrations of the day can influence our tendency to "see" cheating. And remember that our observations always involve inferences about the meaning of the student's actions. Sometimes a person running from the scene of a crime really is going to notify the police. It is possible that the "A-student" copied from the "D-student" and not vice versa. It is not impossible that two students seated next to each other really did choose the same right and wrong answers by sheer chance.

Discussing the possibility of cheating with a test-taker during an examination should be done in a way that does not accuse the person of cheating. Instead of asking a student "Are you cheating?" or immediately confiscating a test, a teacher might say "You may not realize this, but the way you have been looking in that direction makes it appear as if you are looking at another student's paper." Guilty students will recognize this as a warning and may be persuaded to desist; innocent students will understand the possible misinterpretations of their behavior and be grateful for the gentle reminder.

Being guarded in our inferences also involves our ascertaining the likelihood that cheating *did not* occur. A thorough and responsible reaction to a suspicion of cheating requires that a teacher seek out plausible alternative explanations for the situation as vigorously as he or she pursues the potential that a student cheated.

Third, when responding to suspected cheating, remember that *any* response can have an effect on the student suspected—and on many uninvolved students as well. For example, a teacher should understand that the mere accusation of cheating can have a profound effect on a student's self-esteem, willingness to confide in the teacher, and effort on future assignments. It is not unlikely that a student might think, "Why shouldn't I cheat on this? The teacher thinks I'm a cheater anyway."

Or suppose that a teacher discovered that several students passed around answers for a test prior to the examination. However, when questioned, it is not clear which or how many students were involved. Should all students in the class be required to retake the test? Is that response fair to those students who prepared for the test without cheating? Maybe a teacher believes that a student is copying from another student during a test. Should the teacher confront the student during the examination? If so, the teacher should realize that this option carries risks. Asking a test-taker if he or she is cheating can cause an innocent student to become nervous, upset, and unable to give focused attention for the remainder of the period. A disruption caused by the confrontation can also cause anxiety and distraction for the other, uninvolved students. Some students have told me that, in the past, their teachers have taken special pride in tearing up a student's examination in front of the class during a test "as a lesson" to the other students about cheating.

But just ignoring the copying can also be problematic. That option can reinforce a perception that the instructor doesn't care about cheating. Whatever response is chosen, the teacher should remember not to get "tunnel vision" about the incident, but must consider how any intervention will affect all students.

Fourth, responding to cheating requires gathering and maintaining any evidence. If found, a cheat sheet should be retained. Any test materials should be copied and retained, including the test materials of any student whose work might have been copied. If plagiarism is suspected, the teacher should make copies of the suspected plagiarist's paper, the suspected victim's paper, or any source material believed to have been plagiarized. Develop a written record to help document the event and to serve as a memory aid in the future. The record should consist of notes regarding the day, time, location, and details of the incident; any discussion with the student or others; and any actions you took or other relevant observations.

Fifth, do not proceed alone. It is important to involve other professionals when responding to cheating. For example, it is often wise to ask a colleague to examine any evidence for a "second opinion" regarding whether cheating has occurred. When confronting a student about suspicions, it is sometimes prudent to have another teacher, school counselor, administrator, or other person in attendance. The colleague can help prevent a situation from becoming inflammatory; he or she can attest to the veracity of any facts should confirmation be necessary in the future.

Sixth, as part of responding to cheating, a teacher will have collected evidence from students suspected of cheating as well as supporting evidence from those who may not have cheated or who may have been innocent victims. Subsequently, the teacher may have involvement with other teachers or administrators regarding the situation. In any event, all parties involved are entitled to confidentiality in the matter. Until (and perhaps after) the matter has been resolved, all student materials should be retained in a secure location and the teacher should refrain from discussing the matter with anyone but those with a need to be involved. As a precaution, even when others are involved, it is a good idea to redact the names or other identifying information from students' work so that a student suspected of cheating is not harmed should the suspicions turn out to be false.

Seventh, any punishment meted out in response to cheating should fit the crime. In most cases, teachers themselves must make the final determination regarding what sanction to invoke if a student has cheated. There are no firm "sentencing guidelines" that can be offered, and school district policies may offer only the most vague prescriptions. However, one sensible principle is that the seriousness of the cheating should be related to the severity of the disciplinary measures taken. Does cheating on a brief quiz merit a failing grade on the unit? For the semester? Should a student get no credit for failing to have an accurate bibliography for a term paper, or would requiring the student to complete a tutorial on plagiarism and requiring him or her to redo the assignment be more appropriate? Do some instances of first-time cheating merely warrant a warning? What kinds of responses to similar situations have other teachers found to be appropriate?

Finally, related to this advice is a second principle. It is best to have in mind some response ahead of time and to apply any response fairly and uniformly in similar situations. For example, a teacher may have a written or spoken policy announced to the class that cheating will result in no credit for an assignment. It is always preferable to handle difficult situations in a systematic, planned way as opposed to being seen as capricious.

Conclusions

Kenneth Eble is a respected researcher and author on the skills that teachers need to be successful in the classroom. One of his books, *The Craft of Teaching*, covers many areas related to instructional planning, design, and delivery. One of the topics Eble addresses is the problem of cheating. He describes the teacher's role in responding to cheating as part of "the grubby stuff and dirty work" (1998, p. 123) of teaching.

Indeed, I don't believe that any teacher who has had an occasion to deal with cheating would remember the incident fondly. At best, responding to cheating is a task with few rewards and many potential pitfalls. Many teachers simply avoid it.

However, as Eble notes, responding to cheating is part—albeit an undesirable part—of the teaching profession. Those who administer tests, who give assignments, who grade papers, and who generally serve as a model for students have certain professional obligations. These include ensuring fairness in testing and grading, protecting students who do not cheat, correcting students who do cheat, and modeling high ethical standards.

As we have seen in this chapter, responding to cheating is difficult and time-consuming, and teachers who respond may subject themselves to professional approbation or worse. It can take courage and determination to engage in the grubby stuff.

On a brighter note, there is help for those educators who take on their full array of professional responsibilities. Awareness of the methods students use to cheat on tests and to plagiarize work for a term paper or written assignment is a first step toward being able to identify cheating. There are specific things that teachers can do to detect cheating in these situations. When reacting to cheating, following appropriate guidelines will help protect the teacher as well as all students from many unwanted or unforeseen consequences of responding to cheating. And, as we will see in the next chapter, there are a number of strategies to prevent cheating that can help all concerned to minimize the chances of cheating occurring at all.

Questions for Further Discussion

What are some strategies that you use to detect cheating in your classroom? Which of those strategies do you think . . .

Is the most effective? Why?

Is the least effective? Why?

Compared with your comfort with and ability to use technology to detect cheating, how comfortable and capable do you think your students are in using technology to their advantage?

Go to one or more of the Web sites that students might use to help them cheat (see Resource B). What is your reaction to the content, sophistication, accuracy, and availability of what you find there?

Try out one or more of the high-tech ways of detecting cheating described in this chapter or listed in Resource C. How would you rate the relevance, sophistication, and ease of use of what you find there?

Are there factors that dissuade you from becoming involved in detecting and responding to cheating? What are they? What, if anything, would help to remove some of those barriers?

Do you have a personal experience responding to cheating? What did you learn from that experience that you would offer as advice to another educator?

CHAPTER 5

How Can Cheating Be Prevented?

I n Chapter 1, we saw that students cheat primarily to obtain higher grades. Simple enough. Unfortunately, preventing cheating is not as simple as understanding why it occurs. It is probably true that no strategy represents the silver bullet of prevention. A popular bumper sticker proclaims, "As long as there are tests, there will always be prayer in schools." We could add that there will always be cheating, too.

In this chapter, we look at several prongs that can work together to reduce the incidence of cheating. These strategies range from actions that political bodies can take, such as enacting laws and policies, to actions that educators can take to create a classroom climate that emphasizes accurate assessment for promoting learning, to the nuts and bolts strategies that individual teachers can implement for tests and written assignments. The following ideas can be used individually or in combination as appropriate to the needs of the local situation.

Improving Classroom Assessments, Assignments, and Environments

As we saw in Chapter 1, many of the factors related to student cheating on assignments and tests are not under the teacher's control. A teacher cannot change a student's background, sex, age, GPA, previous achievement, or other background characteristics; it is often challenging to influence a student's motivation, effort, or perceptions about his or her ability or schooling. However, some factors related to cheating *are* under the teacher's control, and there are dozens of ways that teachers can influence the likelihood that students might cheat on a test or plagiarize on a written assignment. Even for students who are intent on cheating, there are ways that teachers can construct assessments and writing exercises so as to reduce the ease with which cheating can be accomplished.

The following sections address some practical, teacher-initiated tips for preventing cheating on tests and plagiarism and for changing the classroom environment so that the risks and motivations for cheating are reduced. The first portion of Resource D also contains a sample that teachers can use as a model to begin crafting their own straightforward guidelines for students regarding cheating on tests and plagiarism.

Practical Tips for Preventing Cheating on Tests

I suspect that most teachers implement some strategies for deterring cheating on tests. Common sense dictates that we don't leave copies of an upcoming test or answer key unattended on our desk while we are out of the classroom. Most of us have taken tests where we were instructed to leave space between ourselves and other test-takers, to cover our answers, and so on. Some of the ideas in the following set of seven specific guidelines may be familiar advice; hopefully, many of these ideas will be helpful in themselves or in stimulating other prevention strategies. A summary of the seven tips is also provided in Table 5.1.

It should also be noted that not all of the strategies listed may even be relevant for all tests. It is reasonable to pay greater or lesser attention to prevention depending on the stakes of the test and the criticality of obtaining accurate information. For example, while Idea Number 2 (Be fair and open about testing) might apply to all situations, Idea Number 5 (Ensure test security) might come into play only for final examinations. Ultimately, each teacher must judge which prevention tips are appropriate for each assessment situation.

Table 5.1   Tips for Preventing Cheating on Tests

1. Address cheating in advance of testing.
2. Be fair and open about testing.
3. Adjust test characteristics.
4. Be serious and attentive during testing.
5. Ensure test security.
6. Provide a secure test environment.
7. Don't encourage cheating.

1. Address Cheating in Advance of Testing. Preventing cheating on tests begins with the teacher taking the lead in acknowledging that the temptation to cheat sometimes exists and stating to the class that he or she takes the matter seriously. Teachers should—before classes begin—decide upon what classroom rules should be in place for testing, what expectations they have for student behavior during tests, what they will do for makeup testing if a student is absent on the day of a test, and what policies they have for students leaving the classroom during a test, marking double answers, wearing baseball caps, and so on. Teachers should also—early in the school year and whenever judged necessary subsequently—inform students of the importance of academic integrity, of what constitutes cheating, and of what the consequences of cheating are. All such information provided to students should be appropriate for their age, grade, prior experiences, and developmental level, and should be approached in a serious but nonthreatening manner.

2. Be Fair and Open About Testing. To the extent possible, teachers should make testing an occasion on which students are prepared to perform as best they can, and to demonstrate their true levels of knowledge, skill, or ability. This means that students should have adequate notice of when tests, quizzes, or exams are scheduled and should be afforded adequate time to prepare. Teachers should fully inform students in advance, as much as is reasonable, regarding the characteristics of a test and the testing process, such as how many questions there will be; the format they will be in; the time constraints that will apply; the topics, units, chapters, or objectives the test will cover; how the tests will be scored or graded; and how the student's test performance will figure into his or her overall grade. Teachers should also give students practice using any unfamiliar materials or procedures that will be required for successful performance on the test, as well as practice with any unfamiliar test question format or response requirement.

3. Adjust Test Characteristics (As Appropriate). Some characteristics of tests just seem to provide enhanced opportunity or ease of cheating. For example, it is easy to signal the answers to multiple-choice questions or to see at a glance which response a neighboring classmate has circled on his or her test. A **test form** with a space along the left margin with short lines on which students are to write their answers can make finding the location of an answer on a classmate's paper even easier. On the other hand, some test question formats make cheating more difficult. For example, it is difficult to signal the correct response when a constructed-response **item format** is used (e.g., fill-in-the-blank, short answer); it is nearly impossible to peek at a classmate's paper and copy the entire answer to an essay question. In addition, the use of two or more different tests (i.e., alternate forms) within a class can further reduce the potential for successful copying.

4. Be Serious and Attentive During Testing. I recall a high school course of my own in which cheating on tests was rampant. It is admittedly a stereotype, but the teacher for this particular course was also a coach for one of the high school sports teams. Too often, the time he spent giving a test was time he spent in his familiar chair, fixed in the corner of the room, catching up on book work related to his coaching duties, reading the sports section of a newspaper or a sports-related magazine, or simply kicking back and taking a break from all of his duties. Predictably, while he rested his eyes, we strained ours.

The time that students spend taking tests is just as important as any other class time for a teacher to be "on duty." From a pedagogical perspective, the time that students are working on a test is a time that a teacher can be circulating around the room, responding to students' concerns, clarifying test questions, making sure that each student understands the tasks, is on the right page, and so on. From an assessment perspective, a teacher can gather good information during this time regarding how difficult the students are finding the test to be, whether the time allotted was appropriate, whether some test questions were ambiguous or confusing, and so forth. This time should also be spent monitoring test-takers as part of discouraging cheating. A teacher who is conscientious about answering students' questions and proctoring during a test communicates that he or she is serious both about helping students and about integrity in the classroom.

5. Ensure Test Security. Ensuring test security sounds like it involves a police detail, but it only means that teachers should be alert for possible misuse of test materials so that we can have confidence that a test we administer will yield accurate information about student learning.

Paying attention to test security means that teachers may need to create multiple versions of a test. They should avoid reusing the same test for first and second period students, or reusing any test in this year's class that was administered last year. It means that teachers should avoid relying on publisher-provided test banks, tests photocopied or duplicated from a teacher's manual, or other sources that can easily be obtained by students.

Test security also means keeping track of all test materials, including all copies of a printed test. A teacher may want to number tests, or distribute tests to students one at a time, and to account for each copy following a test administration. In addition to reasons involving test security, the Federal Educational Rights and Privacy Act (FERPA) also requires that teachers' records of students' grades be kept confidential, which means that grade books should be kept in a location where students cannot view the grades of other students—or alter their own.

6. *Provide a Secure Test Environment.* Providing a secure test environment means providing each student taking a test with clear guidelines regarding what materials are permitted during the test and an atmosphere that permits each to focus his or her attention on the task at hand—which is demonstrating his or her knowledge or skill on the tested content.

The first part of this guideline is primarily for the benefit of the person who will use, interpret, or make a decision based on the student's test score. In this case, providing a secure test environment means that the teacher should arrange the physical space (e.g., such things as location, work area, students' desks, and student seating) in a way that minimizes the opportunities for students to cheat. The familiar practice of having students leave an empty desk between them when seating themselves for a test is a common way to deter cheating. Providing a safe location for students to leave their backpacks, purses, notebooks, or other items that are either not necessary or not permitted during a test is another good idea.

The second part of the guideline—providing an atmosphere that permits students to focus on the test—aids the teacher in terms of obtaining an accurate idea about each student's achievement, but indirectly. The following illustration and recommendation goes against much of the "conventional wisdom" but—I believe—is in line with good testing practice.

Most of us are probably familiar with the common advice that students keep their papers covered during a test to prevent other students from cheating. In fact, when I was an elementary school student, each of us actually had a special sheet of paper that we used during a test as a cover sheet. The sheet of paper on which we wrote our answers was to be kept covered at all times, save for a brief moment when we were going to record our answer to a question. Then, we would move the cover sheet just enough to reveal the space for recording an answer; we would write down our response quickly; then we would hurriedly replace the cover sheet.

This practice may have in fact prevented some cheating. However, I believe that it may be a bad idea for a couple of reasons. First, it can communicate to students that cheating is all around them, and that it is their responsibility to prevent other students from cheating, or at least not to present a temptation. In fact, on any particular test, few students are likely to cheat, and the primary responsibility for preventing cheating rests with the person who is giving the test—the teacher. Second, this practice can induce anxiety in students and, at minimum, can cause them to be distracted from the task at hand and from demonstrating their real mastery of whatever the test is attempting to assess.

It is probably the case that, in some situations, the teacher may need to enlist the students' aid in preventing cheating by requiring the use of cover sheets (such as when the classroom is cramped). However, less burdensome (for the student, at least) and equally effective techniques exist, such as alternate forms of a test, or even the same test form with questions in different, scrambled orders. Overall, it should be remembered that it is primarily the teacher's role to ensure a secure test environment, one in which all students feel secure and undistracted so that they can obtain a fair assessment of their learning.

7. Don't Encourage Cheating. This last bit of advice for preventing cheating on tests might sound ridiculous. However, some teachers actually (and unwittingly) encourage cheating.

One common way that teachers do this is by having unreasonable grading standards. In my own experience (and probably that of many readers) I have had instructors who announce during the first week of classes that they use a very stringent grading scale: "I can tell you right now that I've only given one A in 32 years of teaching." Or teachers use a norm-referenced grading scale (the top 10% get As, the next 20% get Bs, the middle 40% get Cs, 20% will get Ds, and the lowest 10% will get Fs). When all students work hard and learn much, such a norm-referenced grading system is often perceived by students as "unfair" (because, well, it *is* unfair) and can actually be an incentive to compete and cheat. Finally, I've heard teachers actually attempt to "motivate" students with the specter of low grades: "I want each of you to look at the student seated to your left and at the student seated to your right; one of them won't make it past the midterm. Will it be you?" Students, with some good cause, interpret those kinds of motivational speeches as a justification to cheat.

Teachers can also unwittingly encourage cheating by failing to pay attention to the other circumstances that students face. For example, in elementary schools, many teachers give tests on Fridays. Why is that? It seems hard for me to believe that each unit of each subject is so carefully synchronized, and that each unit was so meticulously planned, and that instruction has gone so swimmingly well that it just happens that all tests are given on Fridays. This kind of scheduling places enormous pressure on students to prepare for many tests simultaneously. When faced with Thursday afternoon soccer practice, Thursday night youth group meeting, and five tests to prepare for the next day, the rationalization that "the teacher deserves it if I cheat" is, to some extent, understandable.

Another way that teachers can unintentionally encourage cheating is by relying too heavily on open-book tests. Surely the practice of allowing students to use their books, notes, or other resources when taking a test can be acceptable. The appropriateness of the practice depends, however, on the goals that the teacher has for the testing, the inferences he or she desires to make from the resulting student performances, and the suitability of the test objectives to an open-book format.

For example, open-book tests are ordinarily not appropriate for situations in which the material to be tested targets largely recall or understanding. In such cases, open-book tests can change the inference a teacher can make from "how well my students have learned the content" to "how quickly and accurately my students can locate information."

In many cases, a heavy reliance on open-book testing can also dissuade some students from fully preparing for a test, from studying in advance, or from even reading the required materials. Other students (even those who prepare ardently) have individual characteristics that make them spend inordinate amounts of time on open-book tests—searching, reviewing, and verifying every answer to the point of turning a simple open-book quiz into a rigorous research project. Unless a teacher provides essentially unlimited time on open-book tests, it is possible that the practice inadvertently promotes student behaviors that are not necessarily helpful to them.

And, of course, open-book tests can present opportunities for cheating. The margins of textbooks provide ample room for students to inscribe other information from prohibited sources. When students are allowed to use their books or notes, a teacher can be certain that *only* the students' books and notes were used if the teacher scrutinizes the materials that each student uses—a prospect that seems logistically prohibitive and overly intrusive.

On the other hand, open-book testing should be considered for situations in which the skills tested are of a higher order. More precisely, open-book testing is most appropriate when the books, notes, or other materials permitted during testing serve as resources or references *for students who know what they are looking for* and *when they know how to find it*. For example, it may not be the intent of the teacher to test whether students have memorized the formula for converting temperatures from Fahrenheit to Celsius. The teacher may, however, be interested in inferring that students can perform such conversions. In such a case—and many others like it—it seems appropriate to permit students to use their books or notes to locate formulas or other relevant fundamental information.

As another example, consider the use of an open-book format for answering an essay question on what the U.S. economic policy should be toward Mexico. It seems that a student would *not* need to have memorized the date of the passage of the North American Free Trade Agreement (NAFTA), the Gross Domestic Products (GDPs) of Mexico, Canada, and the United States, or other facts that could be used in support of the student's position. An open-book or open-note format would be appropriate since, in the course of preparing a response to the essay question, a highly knowledgeable student would use his or her book or notes as resources for supporting material and would incorporate the information into an original thesis. A less knowledgeable student might rely more heavily on including facts, dates, or content from the resources than on conceiving and communicating an original argument in the response. Thus, the open-book resources would not be helpful to either student in actually performing the skill of analysis that the question was intended to elicit. In an ironic way, then, it can be seen that the practice of open-book testing is probably most appropriate when it is least helpful.

Finally, I am going to offer one suggestion that again goes against conventional wisdom. Teachers should avoid giving "take-home" tests accompanied by rules that instruct students to take the test as if it were a secure, in-class test. For example, sometimes teachers assign a take-home test and tell students that they may spend only two hours on the test; they may not use any books or other resources; they may not discuss or work on the test with a classmate; and so on. There are two major problems with this kind of arrangement. I have informally interviewed many high school students about this. Trust me: None of them follow these rules. As soon as the test gets home, the books come out. Second, the only students who follow the rules are the few students who are scrupulously honest. Ironically, in a situation where nearly everyone else ignores the instructions, the honest students are penalized because it is only their performance on the test that is less than it could have been. Under these circumstances—and especially as students who are trying to be honest find out the extent of cheating—it is easy to see that they may to become cynical and adapt their actions to what they see around them.

In all, it is probably best to avoid take-home tests altogether. Take-home tests with strict rules only encourage cheating. By allowing students to take a test at home, the teacher also misses out on many opportunities to interact with students as they are working on the test, to learn of common misunderstandings, or to see how students perceive the test. If a teacher decides to give a take-home test, the best practice is to place a few reasonable restrictions on the students. Allowing students to use their books, notes, and even to collaborate with their peers is reasonable—if only because they are going to do it anyway.

Practical Tips for Preventing Plagiarism

Some of the ideas for preventing plagiarism are identical to those just presented for preventing cheating on tests. For example, Idea Number 1 from the previous list (Address cheating in advance) applies equally to cheating on tests and to plagiarism on written assignments. However, precisely *how* a teacher would prepare students in advance to help them avoid inappropriate actions in their written work is different—and perhaps more complicated—than how a teacher would address behavior appropriate to deterring cheating on tests. The following sections provide a list of practical suggestions tailored to deterring plagiarism. A brief summary of the suggestions is displayed in Table 5.2.

1. Address Plagiarism in Advance. Sneaking a crib sheet into a test or looking at another student's paper during a test just seems to *feel* awkward to most students, and they have an intuitive sense that what they are doing is wrong. However, turning in a written assignment that is the product of cutting and pasting large blocks of text from a Web site often does not produce the same intuitive feeling of breaking the rules. In fact, it can often seem as natural as any other word processing task. Unlike other kinds of cheating, the concept of plagiarism is not familiar to many students and the skill of avoiding plagiarism often needs to be taught. I suspect that students are often telling the truth when they claim that they didn't know there was anything wrong with how they drafted a written assignment.

In fact, research has found that even college undergraduates have little prior knowledge about plagiarism. For one such study, Roig (1997) developed the *Plagiarism Knowledge Survey* (PKS). The PKS

Table 5.2   Tips for Preventing Plagiarism on Written Assignments

1. Address plagiarism in advance.
2. Surprise your students.
3. Teach about related concepts.
4. Structure writing assignments.
5. Consider a developmental approach.
6. Assess the potential for plagiarism.
7. Don't encourage plagiarism.

presents students with an original selection of text followed by several rewritten versions that vary in the degree to which they differ from the original text. Some rewritten versions are blatant plagiarism, some are inappropriate paraphrases, and some are acceptable paraphrases of the original work. Students are instructed to read each of the rewritten versions and decide whether the revision is "Plagiarism," "Not Plagiarism," or "Can't Determine." A student's score is calculated by awarding one point for each rewritten version correctly identified as either plagiarism or not; two points for each rewritten version that could not be identified as either plagiarism or not; and three points for each rewritten version incorrectly identified. Roig administered the PKS to 316 undergraduates in two private colleges. He found that "more than half of the students in our sample were not adequately informed about the proper procedures for paraphrasing text and thus could not correctly distinguish between various types of plagiarized versus correctly paraphrased text" (1997, p. 118).

In short, it would seem that teachers need to make a conscious effort to teach about plagiarism, particularly with less-experienced students at the elementary and secondary school levels. Students need a concrete definition of the concept. They need to hear arguments for why plagiarism is wrong. They can benefit from seeing specific examples of plagiarized text or an unacceptable paraphrase and an explanation regarding what makes it so. (For some excellent sources of such examples, see the descriptions of various materials in Resource C.) Conversely, students should also be taught appropriate referencing, citing, footnoting, and preparing a bibliography. They should be specifically instructed in the proper use of quotation marks.

Finally, at the beginning of a school year or whenever it is appropriate, students should be exposed to the teacher's and/or the school district's official policy on plagiarism. The consequences for violating these policies should be thought out and spelled out in advance.

2. Surprise Your Students. Let's face it. Many of our students think of us, their teachers, as dorks. We may be thought of as OK people, but we are also usually considered to be "out of the loop" on most cutting-edge cultural knowledge, technological innovations, and social trends.

It might come as a shock to students that their teacher knows that term paper download sites exist. Almost surely it will surprise them that software and Web sites are available to help teachers detect plagiarism (see Resource C). So, teachers should visit a site or two. Maybe download a paper. Show students the downloaded document during a presentation on plagiarism and use the document to demonstrate how it can be identified as inauthentic by demonstrating a plagiarism detection site.

Teachers should also get to know their students and their writing. It might also surprise some students that their teacher actually knows them well enough to detect a student's "voice" in a sample of writing, or that the teacher can tell with reasonable certainty whether a student's writing is authentic by the vocabulary, expressions, style, or organization the student uses.

3. Teach About Related Concepts. In addition to teaching directly about plagiarism, it can be prevented by helping students to learn other content and skills. With the advent (and demise) of Napster, some students learned that it is variously easier (or harder) to obtain free music over the Internet. Few students probably understand much about the principles of "fair use," or copyright, or intellectual property that underlie current debates about how emerging technologies can or should be used. The content of a teacher-directed discussion or lesson on the meaning of copyright would be new territory for many students.

Students are also rarely given the tools with which to evaluate the quality and appropriate use of Web resources. For that matter, for many students the notion that material on the Internet is not all of equal quality is foreign. In previous times, students needed to learn to be critical consumers of information in print ("You can't believe everything you see in the papers"); today's students need to acquire the same analytical skills for information obtained via electronic sources.

4. Structure Writing Assignments. A very pragmatic way of preventing plagiarism is to structure the written assignment so as to make it difficult to plagiarize. For example, instead of letting students choose their own topics for a term paper, the teacher could assign topics. Or students could each propose two or three topics; the topics could be written on slips of paper and placed in a jar so students could select a topic at random from the jar.

If a teacher does assign topics, the best strategy here includes assigning topics that are sufficiently narrow, unique, or locally relevant so that there is little chance that students will find a prewritten paper on the topic. Teachers should also vary topics over semesters and years so that essays written by students in previous classes cannot be recycled.

When teachers do not assign topics, they can still mandate certain formats or other requirements that make plagiarism less likely. For example, in one of my courses, I require that certain aspects of a topic be covered, in a certain order, and using specific subheadings to organize the paper. It is highly unlikely that any prewritten paper will comport with these requirements, and the amount of revisions that a student would need to do to get a prewritten paper in the required format would discourage plagiarism and increase the chances that the student would view it as easier to write his or her paper from scratch.

A final idea for helping teachers to dissuade students from plagiarizing is for teachers to pay attention to the sources that students use for a writing assignment. A teacher may wish to mandate that some or all of the sources used be from the school's library, from a provided list of Web sites, and so forth. If a teacher decides not to mandate sources, he or she can still require that students produce an annotated bibliography to accompany their paper, or that students turn in copies of the sources they quoted, printouts of Web pages used, or copies of articles they relied upon to prepare the paper.

5. Consider a Developmental Approach. I'm not an expert in the teaching of writing. I assume that, like many things, the skill of good writing can be acquired in many ways and that there are a number of sound approaches to teaching writing. What I am calling a "developmental" approach may not even be accepted terminology (and probably confirms my outsider status among composition teachers). Readers who are interested in learning more about assessing writing should consult other sources (e.g., Arter & McTighe, 2001).

Nonetheless, it seems to me that teachers could configure writing assignments so that students complete larger assignments in stages. I have tried such a strategy in my own courses and both I and my students often find it helpful. It can also help prevent plagiarism.

Using a developmental approach, a teacher would begin by having students identify a topic. The first product students submit might be a statement of the topic and a brief rationale for why they chose the topic, why they find the topic interesting, and so on. A second phase of the larger assignment could require students to turn in an outline for the paper they propose to write. Through communication and negotiation between teacher and students, either of these first two stages could involve modifications to the proposed topic or outline. The outline could be followed by submission of a rough draft, and eventually, a final version of the paper would be due. By maintaining all of the interim portions of the project (i.e., negotiated topic statement and rationale, proposed outline, rough draft), the teacher may have ample evidence that the eventual final version of a paper truly is an original product of the student's own effort. Conversely, the same paper trail that precedes a totally different final version could suggest that the final version is not the student's own work.

6. *Assess the Potential for Plagiarism.* Other practical strategies for preventing plagiarism include incorporating direct assessment of the potential for plagiarism in a class of students.

For example, one idea that teachers can use to discourage students from relying on cut-and-pasted material for a writing project is to include questions about students' projects on a written examination. If students know that they will also be tested on their written work, they will be less likely to prepare the work cavalierly. Students who cannot answer questions about their own written work have possibly plagiarized its content. And, if this idea does not ensure that students do not plagiarize, it at least increases the possibility that students who do plagiarize will familiarize themselves sufficiently with the written material that they will have learned something about the topic in the process.

Another idea is to incorporate a requirement that a written assignment include a section in which students relate the content of their essays to a personal experience, tie the ideas in the paper to a class discussion, or ground a narrative in a local setting. These kinds of requirements reduce the potential for plagiarism.

Finally, a teacher can directly assess what students know about plagiarism as one way of investigating the potential for plagiarism to occur. An instrument mentioned previously, the *Plagiarism Knowledge Survey,* developed by Miguel Roig, a professor of psychology at St. John's University (Staten Island, New York) for a study of college students, is also available in a lower readability version that would be appropriate for high school students. As with the college version, the test presents students with a definition of plagiarism and a short passage of writing. Then students are given several paraphrased rewritings of the original passage and asked to indicate whether they believe the rewritten version is plagiarism, not plagiarism, or are unclear as to whether it is plagiarism.

The version appropriate for high school students is reproduced in Figure 5.1. Though Roig's instrument is not a test per se (i.e., students would not be graded on it), it can help teachers get a more accurate perception of their students' levels of understanding with respect to plagiarism. At minimum, the instrument can be used as a "conversation starter" in a class discussion about plagiarism.

Plagiarism is defined as taking others' ideas, text, etc., and using them as one's own. For the purpose of this study, let's assume that you are in the process of writing a paper.

In researching material for the topic you are writing about, you locate the following relevant paragraph in a published source:

> If you have ever had your astrological chart done, you may have been impressed with its seeming accuracy. Careful reading shows many such charts to be made up of mostly flattering traits. Naturally, when your personality is described in desirable terms, it is hard to deny that the description has the "ring of truth." (Coon, 1995, p. 29)

It would be legitimate to include this portion of text in your paper by enclosing it in quotations, and adding the Coon citation at the end of the paragraph just as it appears above, or in the form of a footnote, depending on the style of writing you use (e.g., MLA, APA). However, let's assume that you want to include the information from the Coon paragraph in your paper but that you don't want to use a direct quote as shown above. Instead, you are considering the rewritten versions shown below. How different does the rewritten, paraphrased version have to be so as to not be classified as a case of plagiarism?

Directions:

What follows are several rewritten paragraphs. Examine each rewritten paragraph carefully, compare it with the original version, and circle the appropriate abbreviation to indicate your judgment about whether the rewritten version constitutes plagiarism or not. Circle P if you believe the revision represents plagiarism; circle NP if you believe the revision is not plagiarism (that is, if you believe the paragraph has been appropriately paraphrased); circle CD if you cannot determine whether the rewritten version is plagiarism or not. Please indicate the reasons for your decision in the space provided. Also, in making your decision, assume that a correct citation (e.g., a footnote; Coon, 1995) appears in the rewritten version and in the paper's reference section or bibliography in accordance with the specific writing style used in your profession.

Paraphrase #1

> Naturally, when your personality is described in desirable terms, it is hard to deny that the description has the "ring of truth." If you have ever had your astrological chart done, you may have been impressed with its seeming accuracy. Careful reading shows many such charts to be made up of mostly flattering traits.

Circle One: P NP CD
Reason: _____

_____

Figure 5.1   Plagiarism Knowledge Survey

Notes: From M. Roig (n.d.). Used by permission. Available upon request from roigm@stjohns.edu. Correct answers are "P" for Paraphrases 1 through 4, NP for Paraphrases 5 and 6. Scores are determined by awarding one point for each rewritten version correctly identified as either plagiarism or not; two points for each rewritten version that could not be identified as either plagiarism or not; and three points for each rewritten version incorrectly identified. Scores can range from 10 to 30 with higher scores indicating less knowledge of plagiarism.

Paraphrase #2

If you ever had your astrological chart done, you may have been impressed by how accurate it seemed. A careful reading indicates many such charts to be made up of mainly flattering traits. Of course, when your personality is described in desirable terms, it is hard to deny that the description has the 'ring of truth.'

Circle One: P NP CD

Reason: _____

Paraphrase #3

If you have ever had your astrological chart done, you were probably impressed by how accurate it seemed. A careful reading indicates many such charts to be made up of mainly flattering traits. Of course, it is hard to deny that the description has the 'ring of truth', when your personality is described in desirable terms.

Circle One: P NP CD

Reason: _____

Paraphrase #4

According to Coon, if you ever have had your astrological chart done, you were probably impressed by how accurate it seemed. A careful reading indicates many such charts to be made up of mainly flattering traits. Of course, it is hard to deny that the description has the 'ring of truth' when your personality is described in desirable terms.

Circle One: P NP CD

Reason: _____

Paraphrase # 5

According to Coon, individuals who have had their astrological chart profiled may have been swayed by their apparent precision. If you study these charts, however, you realize that they are primarily composed of complimentary attributes. Obviously, as Coon notes, when one is described with positive, laudable traits, it is difficult to argue against such a flattering portrait of oneself.

Circle One: P NP CD

Reason: _____

Paraphrase #6

Individuals who have had their astrological chart profiled may have been swayed by their apparent precision. If you study these charts, however, you realize that they are primarily composed of complimentary attributes. Obviously, when one is described with positive, laudable traits, it is difficult to argue against such flattering portrait of oneself.

Circle One: P NP CD

Reason: _____

7. Don't Encourage Plagiarism. The final practical tip for preventing plagiarism is to avoid providing students with reasons for engaging in the behavior. Extensive writing assignments such as term papers should have reasonable deadlines for interim iterations of the project as well as for a final version. As with tests, teachers should be sensitive to the other demands on a student's life—especially demands of other courses—and should avoid assigning a term paper or other lengthy written assignment so that it is due at the same time as other major projects. Lastly, teachers should be sensitive to the prior experiences and achievement of their classes. By avoiding assigning topics that are too sophisticated, too complex, or too unfamiliar to students, teachers can help reduce the chance that, out of frustration, a student will turn to plagiarism as a recourse.

Practical Tips for Improving the Classroom Environment

There are two major strategies that teachers can implement to create a classroom environment in which students are less likely to cheat. One strategy is a practical "Don't"; the other strategy is a less concrete "Do."

1. Don't Use Grades Punitively. There are a number of resources that interested readers can consult for information on how to create a fair grading system that communicates clear information about achievement to students, parents, and others (see, for example, Guskey & Bailey, 2001; Haladyna, 1999). Without exception, experts in the area of student grading recommend that grades not be used in a punitive sense.

When a teacher uses grades as punishment for certain student behaviors, the teacher establishes an adversarial relationship with students in which grades are no longer meaningful to students as indicators of their accomplishment. The punitive use of grades only increases the likelihood that students will lose respect for the evaluation system; consequently, the appeal to students of subverting such a system will also be heightened.

The appropriate use of grades is to indicate the extent to which a student has acquired identified skills, mastered certain **content standards,** or made progress on specific learning goals. In some cases, however, the practice still exists of lowering student achievement grades because of misbehavior in class, student absences, or violations of school rules. I have heard of some teachers who assign all students participating in a group project a lower grade if one member of the group fails to meet a deadline or falls short of expectations for his or her contribution to the group's work. However, if good conduct, attendance, and group participation are considered to be valuable—and most teachers would probably agree that they are—then these characteristics deserve to be measured and reported in their own right, not used to raise or lower a student's achievement grade.

2. Foster Assessment for Learning. Though easier said than done in practice, teachers must constantly remind students (and model for them) the principle that the primary reason for any assessment (i.e., a test, quiz, term paper, etc.) is for the student and the teacher to gain a better understanding of the student's acquisition of important knowledge and skills. Accurate assessment is in the student's best interest.

Another way of thinking about this issue is via a dichotomy that researchers have postulated to represent the perspectives that students bring to an assessment event. On one hand is the perspective referred to as a *grade orientation.* A student with a grade orientation sees the primary purpose of instruction as preparing the student for an assessment on which the tangible result of the student's performance (i.e., his or her grade) is the ultimate prize. A student with a grade orientation participates in class discussions, completes assignments, and puts forth maximal effort on tests, term papers, and so forth, in order to obtain the best prize—a high grade.

When competition for grades is seen as the aim of education, an incubator for cheating exists. According to McCabe, in such a classroom culture,

> Students may come to view cheating from a "we" vs. "them" perspective. "We students need to stick together to overcome the obstacles [to high grades] our teachers and/or administrators keep placing in our way." In this situation, rules on collaboration, plagiarism, and other forms of cheating are viewed as just another hassle by students, and bending the rules a little to overcome such obstacles is acceptable. (2001, p. 43)

On the other hand is the perspective referred to as a *learning orientation.* A student with a learning orientation sees the primary purpose of instruction as helping the student to master processes, acquire valuable information or skill, remedy inaccuracies in previous learning, and build the foundation for future learning. The focus is far less tangible than a grade. A student with a learning orientation participates in class discussions, completes assignments, and puts forth maximal effort on tests, term papers, and so on, in order to obtain an intrinsic reward.

Clearly, fostering a learning orientation is not a simple task. Much work remains to be done by researchers in this area to even discover which strategies best foster a learning orientation. One thing is known, however. Students with a learning orientation are noticeably less likely to cheat (Huss et al., 1993). In the words of a high school student interviewed about the problem of cheating at his school, "If the teacher just takes the time to make sure you actually learn the information, I think that would decrease a lot of cheating" (quoted in McCabe, 1999, p. 686).

It is also true that an educational system in which there is competition for grades necessarily works against fostering a learning orientation in students. Thus, under a system in which grades are assigned, teachers must take affirmative actions to avoid pointing students toward grades and the competition for grades as the aim of education. For example, a teacher who posts examples of student work on a bulletin board should consider posting the work of a student who has demonstrated real effort toward mastering skills or concepts, not simply papers that earned the grade of "A."

Another idea to consider is to avoid assigning grades or deducting points on some formative assignments and assessments. Instead, teachers can provide more instructive feedback, suggestions, and encouragement related to the desired learning goals. Teachers can also allow students to redo assignments for a different grade—especially when the teacher wants the grade to communicate how much progress the student made in the learning process, not simply serve as an indication of the quality of the student's first attempt at some goal.

Finally, teachers can remind students that it is not their score on an assignment that will help them be successful in college, perform on the job, or understand more complex material, but the extent to which they are able to grasp and integrate the matter at hand. Schools can develop "honor rolls" of students who have engaged wholeheartedly in learning, not simply those with the highest scores.

School Policies, Honor Codes, and Law

At the institutional or system level, there are also mechanisms that can serve as reminders of the value of academic integrity and that codify proscriptions against cheating on tests and plagiarism. One such mechanism is the policies adopted by school districts regarding cheating. Some schools have also adopted **honor codes** that bind students to a larger system for promoting integrity. Academic integrity has even become the subject of legislation at the state level. Each of these mechanisms is examined in the following sections.

School Policies

Outside the classroom, there are also strategies for preventing cheating of which teachers (and students) should be aware. To begin with, a school district may have a policy on cheating or academic integrity. Sometimes such a policy can be found only in the district's policy manual. Other times, it is incorporated into a student handbook, teachers' syllabi, or distributed to parents or students during an orientation or during a regular class meeting.

Apparently, policies regarding cheating are unfortunately rare. At least, if they do exist, they are not recognized by those in classrooms. For example, in the study by Brandes (1986) involving classroom teachers in California, 109 staff members in elementary and secondary schools were asked if their school or district had a policy on cheating. Of the elementary staff, 100% indicated that their school or district did not have such a policy; at the high school level, 78.4% said no policy was in place. Although the research did not follow up to determine the accuracy of these perceptions, the point is probably moot. Even if a policy exists in all of a state's school districts, it could not possibly be effective at preventing cheating if no one knows it exists. Thus, it would appear that considerably more effort should begin to be directed at developing and disseminating school policies related to academic integrity.

A model policy should begin by stating the importance of ethical conduct in the scholastic setting and in academic work. The policy itself should then be stated, including a list describing, as specifically as practical, the kinds of actions that would constitute violations of the policy. Finally, the text of the policy should include the consequences that can be levied for violations of the policy. Three such model policies are reproduced in Resource D (one from a middle school, and two policies on plagiarism from a university and a community college).

Educators who are interested in promoting academic integrity may first want to check to see whether their districts have a policy on cheating. If not, a policy can be proposed to the board of education through appropriate administrative channels by a staff member, or often at the request of a parent or school district resident. If a policy exists, it should be examined for the elements just noted.

Honor Codes

Honor codes are another institutional mechanism for preventing cheating on tests, preventing plagiarism, and for generally promoting academic and personal integrity. Honor codes are fairly common at the postsecondary level (for a list of colleges and universities that have honor codes, see www.academicintegrity.org); they are not as common at the elementary and secondary school levels. Increasingly, schools at both levels appear to be considering implementing honor codes, perhaps in response to increasing academic misconduct.

An honor code has been defined as "the proclamation and legislation of the intentions of a community of persons united in mutual agreement to oppose those inclinations and strategies that they might otherwise give in to and adopt to further their individual ends" (Hein, 1982, p. 4). As can be seen from this definition, an honor code is not a set of specific rules or a list of behaviors that are proscribed. Rather, an honor code is usually a brief statement of the rights and responsibilities of *all* members of a learning community. Typically, students and teachers are required to sign, affirm, or otherwise endorse an honor pledge that binds them to the principles of the honor code upon entering the learning community.

An important element of honor codes is that they spread responsibility for upholding academic integrity; under an honor code, students themselves have substantially greater responsibility for maintaining an environment of academic integrity. Because of this, in most contexts where honor codes are in place there is also a corresponding relaxation in the overt measures intended to prevent cheating, such as scrutiny by proctors during examinations.

According to one analyst of honor codes, "a good code provides a means by which institutions educate students and everyone involved in the community about what is acceptable behavior and what is not" (Footer, 1996, p. 20). The means by which the members of a learning community come to a mutual understanding and acceptance of their rights and responsibilities is related to the essential elements of a code. According to Footer, those elements include a list of prohibited behaviors and possible sanctions; primary attention to fundamental fairness; and specification of procedural aspects of the disciplinary process.

Three examples of an honor code are shown in Resource D. The first code shown in Resource D is from Duke University (Durham, NC); this version represents an essential statement of academic integrity. The second code is from the University of Virginia (Charlottesville, VA), an institution whose code has a long history. The third honor code found in Resource D is particularly noteworthy. The material shown for Langley High School (Fairfax County, VA) is one of the few honor codes in place at the elementary or secondary school level. More important, however, is the comprehensiveness and clarity of the code. In fact, the excerpt shown in Resource D combines the essential elements of both an honor code and a cheating policy. The code addresses the rights and responsibilities of the entire learning community—students, teachers, parents, counselors, and administrators. The policy portion of the statement provides concrete definitions of cheating and plagiarism, and gives clear guidance regarding what constitutes an infraction, how to avoid infractions, and the penalties for violations. Any school wishing to develop a model cheating policy and/or honor code would do well to emulate Langley's example.

Despite their prevalence and, in many institutions, long history, the evidence is mixed regarding whether honor codes actually deter cheating. Studies of honor codes have found either small positive effects or no effects on reducing the overall incidence of behaviors such as cheating on tests and plagiarism. In contexts where honor codes have had positive effects, it is also unclear precisely how the presence of a code translates into more honest behavior on the part of students. One possibility is that the presence of an honor code raises the stakes and consequences associated with cheating, so that cheating is simply less frequently reported. However, another more likely possibility seems to be that institutions that enact honor codes highlight academic integrity in ways that other institutions do not. The visibility of the code, the mandate that students read and agree to its principles, and the nearly ubiquitous requirement that students inscribe each test and graded paper they submit with the statement "I pledge that I have neither given nor received any unauthorized assistance on this assignment" likely create an environment where the value and expectation of integrity is constantly affirmed.

Law

Perhaps due to the increasing frequency of cheating on tests and plagiarism, these topics have begun to receive more attention from legislative bodies and the courts. For readers interested in a summary of many of the legal issues involved, Standler (2000) provides an informative and accessible overview.

In response to the proliferation of term paper mills, some states have gone so far as to pass legislation making it against the law to sell term papers, theses, and similar materials. For example, according to the California Education Code,

> No person shall prepare, offer to prepare, cause to be prepared, sell, or otherwise distribute any term paper, thesis, dissertation, or other written material for another person, for a fee or other compensation, with the knowledge, or under circumstances in which he should reasonably have known, that such term paper, thesis, dissertation, or other written material is to be submitted by any other person for academic credit at any public or private

college, university, or other institution of higher learning in this state. (California Education Code, §66400)

According to the Texas Penal Code regarding the "Deceptive Preparation and Marketing of Academic Product," it is a Class C misdemeanor to sell term papers to students at a college or university in the state. According to the Code,

(a) For purposes of this section:
(1) "Academic product" means a term paper, thesis, dissertation, essay, report, recording, work of art, or other written, recorded, pictorial, or artistic product or material submitted or intended to be submitted by a person to satisfy an academic requirement of the person.
(2) "Academic requirement" means a requirement or prerequisite to receive course credit or to complete a course of study or degree, diploma, or certificate program at an institution of higher education.
(b) A person commits an offense if, with intent to make a profit, the person prepares, sells, offers or advertises for sale, or delivers to another person an academic product when the person knows, or should reasonably have known, that a person intends to submit or use the academic product to satisfy an academic requirement of a person other than the person who prepared the product.
(c) A person commits an offense if, with intent to induce another person to enter into an agreement or obligation to obtain or have prepared an academic product, the person knowingly makes or disseminates a written or oral statement that the person will prepare or cause to be prepared an academic product to be sold for use in satisfying an academic requirement of a person other than the person who prepared the product.

In the state of Washington, the selling of term papers is similarly prohibited:

(1) The legislature finds that commercial operations selling term papers, theses, and dissertations encourages academic dishonesty, and in so doing impairs the public confidence in the credibility of institutions of higher education whether in this state or any other to function within their prime mission, that of providing a quality education to the citizens of this or any other state.

(2) The legislature further finds that this problem, beyond the ability of these institutions to control effectively, is a matter of state concern, while at the same time recognizing the need for and the existence of legitimate research functions.

It is the declared intent of RCW 28B.10.580 through 28B.10.584, therefore, that the state of Washington prohibit the preparation for sale or commercial sale of term papers, theses and dissertations: PROVIDED, That such legislation shall not affect legitimate and proper research activities: PROVIDED FURTHER, That such legislation does not impinge on the rights, under the First Amendment, of freedom of speech, of the press, and of distributing information. (Revised Code of Washington, 28B.10.580)

Finally, it is worth noting that some states have also legislated against cheating by teachers themselves. Such cheating occurs, for example, when a teacher inappropriately divulges the contents of a state-mandated examination to students, when the teacher uses inappropriate test preparation methods with students, or when a teacher alters a student's answers. One example of such legislation is found in the Ohio Revised Code, which states that "no person shall reveal to any student any specific question that the person knows is part of a [state-mandated] test . . . or in any other way assist a pupil to cheat on such a test" (§3319.151). In addition to revealing specific questions, a teacher may not engage in

(1) any preparation activity that undermines the reliability and/or validity of inferences drawn from the assessment results;

(2) any practice that results solely in raising scores or performance levels on a specific assessment instrument without simultaneously increasing the student's achievement level as measured by tasks and/or instruments designed to assess the same content domain;

(3) any practice involving the reproduction of actual assessment materials, through any medium, for use in preparing students for an assessment;

(4) any preparation activity that includes questions, graphs, charts, passages, or other materials included in the assessment instrument or in a parallel form of the instrument, and/or materials that are paraphrases or highly similar in content to those in actual use;

(5) preparation for the assessment [that] focuses primarily on the assessment instrument or a parallel form of the

instrument, including its format, rather than on the objectives being assessed;

(6) any practice that does not comply with, or has the appearance of not complying with, statutory and/or regulatory provisions related to security of assessment instruments used in schoolwide or districtwide programs; and

(7) any practice that supports or assists others in conducting unethical or inappropriate preparation activities. (Ohio Revised Code, Sections 3301-7-01, C1-C7)

In Ohio, a violation of these regulations constitutes a misdemeanor and results in a mandatory one-year suspension of the offender's teaching license and possible termination.

Conclusions

A number of suggestions for preventing cheating on tests and plagiarism in written assignments have been presented in this chapter. These ideas range from concrete steps that a teacher can take when conceptualizing a test or written assignment to broader policy measures and laws that can be enacted by school boards and legislatures. Resources at the end of this book also list organizations, Web sites, and other resources for detecting and preventing cheating, as well as model policies that can be implemented to focus the attention of both students and educators on the definition and value of integrity in the classroom.

In reality, the prevention of cheating is necessarily multifaceted. The most effective course of prevention probably entails some combination of all of the suggestions mentioned. As we will see in the concluding chapter, however, one superordinate idea not addressed in this chapter may actually be the most effective: our ability to perceive and reject fundamentally unsound approaches to dealing with cheating and our willingness to actually commit ourselves to classroom environments where integrity rules.

Questions for Further Discussion

What kinds of things do you tell students in your classroom about cheating? What are some key ideas that you try to communicate to them either explicitly or by example?

What strategies do you use to help prevent cheating on tests? Which of them would you say is the most effective? Why? Which is the least effective? Why?

What strategies do you use to help prevent plagiarism? Which of them would you say is the most effective? Why? Which is the least effective? Why?

Find out if your school district has a policy on cheating.

> If so, how would you rate it on each of the following criteria: clarity, fairness, and usefulness? What aspects, if any, of the policy do you think should be changed? Why?

> If not, do you think such a policy is needed in your district? Why or why not? Are there unique problems or circumstances in your district that a cheating policy should address?

What is your classroom grading system? Do you think that your approach to grading is fair? What characteristics make it so? Are some students critical of your approach to grading, or do they think some aspects are unfair? Why?

Does your school district have an honor code? If so, how clear, fair, and effective do you think the code is? If not, do you think that an honor code would work in your district? Why or why not?

CHAPTER 6

What Are the Next Steps?

Throughout the preceding chapters of this book, I've tried to restrain myself from editorializing or from injecting much personal opinion or bias into the treatment of cheating. I suppose it goes without saying that I think that promoting academic integrity is a good thing; the very act of writing a book about a topic is probably a clear indication that an author has some passion and subjectivity about it. By and large, though, I've tried to report objectively about what the research has to say about cheating, about what we know can be done to detect and prevent it, and so on. For the most part, I've tried to stick to a "just the facts, ma'am" approach.

Well, no more Mister Nice Guy.

In this chapter, I try to summarize some of what we've learned from the previous chapters. I'll also try to present some specific recommendations for how we might proceed to address the problem of cheating if, having read this book, you are convinced that something could and should be done. First, though, I'd like to step away from a more careful and somewhat measured approach to state with some passion what I think should *not* be done.

A Really Dumb Idea

If the section heading above reads, "A Really Dumb Idea," that means that the editors at the publisher of this book, Corwin Press, have let me push the boundaries of appropriate language for a serious publication. If some other heading is there, then it means that I've had to label one really dumb idea for addressing cheating in some other, more delicate way. The truth is, though, that I can't think of a more apt or succinct description for one of the more popular ideas that can be heard floating around for how to respond to cheating.

In essence, the argument and wrongheaded recommendation about how to address the problem of cheating goes something like this: The American educational system uses grades as one way of helping to make decisions about students. For example, grades are frequently used as part of promotion or retention decisions, graduation decisions, scholarship decisions, placement and admissions decisions, and so on. Grades are assigned on the work students do on graded assignments and tests. Because grades are related to the important decisions just mentioned and other consequences, students are tempted to cheat. If there were no grades, students would not cheat. Therefore, we should do away with high stakes assignments, tests, grades, or all of the above.

That is a dumb idea for several reasons, and clearly not the right approach to addressing cheating.

To begin with, the entire rationale ignores that grades—or some system of easily communicated, defensible, and objective evaluation—are necessary components of educational decision making. We make decisions all the time in education—decisions that place students into categories such as pass or fail, promote or retain, or Basic, Proficient, and Advanced. Even the common grading system of A, B, C, D, and F essentially involves placing students into one of five categories. The need to make categorical decisions might seem obvious, but a well-reasoned rationale bears explication, and I (and others) have tried to provide as much in other places.

For example, in Mehrens and Cizek (2001, Chap. 19), we provide an argument to support the position that there is no way to escape making categorical decisions. If, for example, some students graduate from high school and others do not—based on grades, test scores, or whatever—a categorical decision has been made. Clearly we'd like all students to graduate, but we'd also like whatever information is used to inform that decision to be of high quality. However, if we can conceive of achievement so poor that the student should not receive a diploma, then theoretically a cutoff exists, and a categorical decision-making process is in place. Categorical decisions are unavoidable, and they are also observable and accepted in many situations. High school music teachers make such decisions as who should be first chair for the clarinets. College faculty members make decisions to tenure (or not) their colleagues. In the United States we embrace categorical decision making regarding who should be licensed to practice medicine.

In the final analysis, it seems axiomatic to conclude that categorical decisions must be made in education and many other arenas. And as long as any categorical decisions must be made, most people would prefer an openness surrounding the sources of information used to make the decisions and that the information used has the characteristics of being dependable (what measurement specialists refer to as *reliability*) and accurate (what is called *validity*). Tests, graded assignments, and marking systems are good ideas when the information they yield helps us to make better, more defensible decisions about students. Doing away with tests, written assignments, grades, and so on would be a wise response to addressing cheating only if more dependable and accurate processes were waiting in the wings to replace those currently used. For better or worse, however, that's not currently the case. Doing away with those things we currently use to help make decisions about students might lessen the incidence of cheating by students. It would also lessen the incidence of good decisions for students. That's a dumb idea.

It is interesting to note that the logic of addressing cheating by eliminating the competition for grades; the ranking, categorizing, or evaluating of students; or the decisions made about students is made only in the context of education. For example, businesses cheat all the time in a free market economy; we don't recommend doing away with commerce. Athletes cheat to gain an advantage in nearly all sports; we don't react by suggesting that the Super Bowl, the Olympics, or Little League baseball be eliminated. The fact that husbands cheat on their wives (or vice versa) is an obviously ridiculous justification for doing away with marriage. (I suppose that because people cheat on their taxes, I could support doing away with the IRS, but that's the only counterexample I can think of.) In short, while it is true that students are almost certain to cheat as long as there are tests, written assignments to be evaluated, grades, and decisions to be made, those facts are not logically related to the proposed solution of doing away with those things as a legitimate strategy for dealing with cheating.

A related (and equally bad) idea involves a compromise of sorts. Some people would address cheating by tolerating grades, tests, and so on, but they would remove the consequences associated with them. In essence, the argument is quite similar to other arguments about categorical decisions. This specific version focuses on the **"high stakes"** nature of categorical decisions and suggests that if the stakes were lower, cheating would be eliminated. That strategy won't work either, and there is even research support to refute it.

A recent article in the *American School Boards Journal* described the action research project of Sharon Jones, a counselor at Rigby High School (Rigby, ID). Apparently the counselor was curious about whether young students would engage in cheating as easily as it appears that high school students do. So, according to the article,

> [Ms. Jones] visited two second-grade classes and two fifth-grade classes. She gave them spelling words to study and told them they would be tested on the words the next day. In one second-grade class and one fifth-grade class, she told the students that anyone who spelled all the words correctly or made only one mistake would receive a candy bar. No candy bars were offered to students in the other two classes.
>
> Jones collected the tests and graded them but didn't mark her grades on the papers. The next day she asked the students to grade their own papers, and then she compared the students' grades with the grades she had assigned. Among the second-graders and fifth-graders in classes that were not offered candy bars, only one kid cheated by changing wrong answers to correct ones. In the other two classes, all but three kids cheated just to get the candy bar.
>
> Looking beyond spelling tests and candy bars, Jones concluded: "Students will cheat if the stakes are high." (Bushweller, 1999, p. 27)

If the stakes are high? This account demonstrates that reducing or eliminating the importance (i.e., the stakes) associated with tests, grades, or assignments with consequences is not likely to be an effective way of dealing with cheating. It is difficult to imagine any *lower* stakes than in this situation. I'm not sure of one detail of Jones's study, but as a research project, the standards for the protection of human participants would almost certainly guarantee that no student received a real grade on the spelling quiz, nor would they have been deceived into thinking that the quiz was "high-stakes." By my reckoning, if second graders in rural Rigby, Idaho (969 families, total population = 2,681), will cheat on a no-stakes spelling quiz for a candy bar, then virtually no amount of lessening the stakes associated with tests, grades, and so forth is going to help make noticeable progress in addressing cheating in any foreseeable educational contexts.

Another Red Herring

A related—and equally wrongheaded—notion is that grades or test scores are overemphasized in situations in which assessment information or grades are used as a sole piece of information for making a decision. It is reasonable advice to suggest that no important decision about a student should be made on the basis of a single test score, and many groups and associations related to the education profession have endorsed such a position.

I, too, think that the foregoing is generally good advice in the field of education but, to be honest, I can see equally reasonable exceptions. For example, I could imagine students who are taking their driver's education course at the local high school. The course consists of two parts: a first section of the course in which students must demonstrate on a written test that they can identify various road signs, that they know certain fundamental driving laws, that they can distinguish between the accelerator and the brake pedal, and so on; and a second part in which each student is allowed to drive while supervised on the public roads. Students are required to pass both portions in order to obtain a driver's license. Because getting a driver's license is a fairly important part of being able to function in modern life, I'd say that the decision regarding whether a student is allowed to progress through each stage of the training program could be considered "high stakes." That reality notwithstanding, I would be willing to use a score on that single test of knowledge to prohibit a student from graduating to the road experience portion of the driver's education course. In fact, state drivers' licensure agencies deny drivers' licenses based on a single test score all the time, and we are all probably safer because of it. If pressed, perhaps we could all think of other such examples of when it is reasonable to rely on a single piece of information for making important decisions.

Nonetheless, in almost every context, the assertion that any educational decision is based on a single grade from an assignment or on a single test score is simply a straw man. As I have explained in another place (see Cizek, 2001), there is a straightforward but accurate response to the assertion of a single measure used for making important decisions such as awarding high school diplomas: It's not true now and probably never has been.

For example, consider the case of the important decision to award or withhold a high school diploma; this context is one in which a "high-stakes" test is often used and purportedly misused as the single bit of information for making the decision. The reality is that multiple sources of information are used, and success on each of them is necessary. In the previously cited work, I surveyed the posted graduation requirements for several states across the United States, and I looked into what the local school district in my area, Chapel Hill, North Carolina, required (see Cizek, 2001). It turned out that nearly every state has a number of hurdles that must be overcome in order to be awarded a diploma. These included course or credit hour require-ments, such as those for Wisconsin's students:

> (a) Except as provided in par. (d), a school board may not grant a high school diploma to any pupil unless the pupil has earned: In the high school grades, at least 4 credits of English including writing composition, 3 credits of social studies including state and local government, 2 credits of mathematics, 2 credits of science and 1.5 credits of physical education; in grades 7 to 12, at least 0.5 credit of health education. (Wisconsin Statutes, Section 118.33, a, 1-2)

Beyond simple course requirements, Pennsylvania—like many states—includes a test performance requirement:

> Each school district, including charter schools, shall specify requirements for graduation in the strategic plan under §4.13. . . . Requirements shall include course completion and grades, completion of a culminating project, and results of local assessments aligned with the academic standards. Beginning in the 2002-2003 school year, students shall demonstrate profi-ciency in reading, writing and mathematics on either the State assessments administered in grade 11 or 12 or local assessment aligned with academic standards and State assessments under §4.52 (relating to local assessment system) at the proficient level or better in order to graduate. (22 PA Code, § 4.24, a)

In addition, not only are highly specific course requirements and test performance mandated in order for students to obtain a high school diploma, but states often have other requirements, such as grades, attendance, and so on. For example, Florida law requires that

> Each district school board shall establish standards for gradua-tion from its schools, and these standards must include . . . achievement of a cumulative grade point average of 1.5 on a 4.0 scale, or its equivalent, for students entering 9th grade before the 1997-1998 school year; however, these students must earn a cumulative grade point average of 2.0 on a 4.0 scale, or its equivalent, in the courses required by subsection (1) that are taken after July 1, 1997, or have an overall cumulative grade

point average of 2.0 or above. (Florida Statutes, Title XVI, S232.246, 5, c)

Finally, as mentioned previously, most states permit local school boards to add to the graduation requirements imposed by the state. In the school district serving the area of Chapel Hill, North Carolina, the requirements include 50 hours of community service learning experience and a limit on the number of days a senior can be absent. Though variability across states and local districts surely exists, the picture is clear: Just one too few days attendance? No diploma. Didn't take American Government? No diploma. Not enough course credits? No diploma. Miss too many questions on a test? No diploma. The same situation exists for nearly all educational decisions. No university makes admissions decisions solely on high school grades, but takes into account SAT scores, letters of recommendation, rigor of a student's high school curriculum, and so on. No school psychologist refers a student for special education services because the student acted out in class one day. No teacher assigns a student to a reading group based solely on listening to the student read aloud for a few minutes. In all of these cases, multiple sources of high-quality information are (or should be) brought to bear in the decision-making process.

In summary, several conclusions about what *not* to do about cheating should be obvious. First, following the suggestion to abolish assessment or grades as a way to "fix" the problem of cheating would only lead to other, greater problems. There will always be some mechanism for making educational decisions and as long as decisions are made, students are likely to be motivated to engage in strategies—legitimate and illegitimate—to make the decisions fall in their favor. To suggest that cheating is caused by the importance of any "single measure" for making decisions reveals a misunderstanding about how educational decisions are made. And, as we have seen in Chapter 4, ignoring cheating is not an effective strategy for dealing with the problem either.

Whew. Now I've gotten those things off my chest. Hopefully, it is clear what we should *not* do to address cheating. I'll get down off the soapbox now and take a less passionate look at what the next essential steps are that can be taken by those interested in addressing the problem.

The Real Challenges and Opportunities

The problem of cheating is one of those "good news, bad news" situations. The bad news is that cheating is prevalent, harmful, misunderstood, sometimes difficult to detect, apparently increasing, and often tolerated. The good news is that educators have a number of effective means for preventing cheating.

A number of practical suggestions for preventing cheating on tests and plagiarism in written assignments were presented in the previous chapter. The Resources at the end of this book also list organizations, Web sites, and other resources for detecting and preventing cheating, as well as model policies that can be implemented to focus the attention of both students and educators on the definition and value of integrity in the classroom. All that is needed now is for those on the front lines to actually commit to changing classroom policies, practices, and environments and to muster the will to become involved.

In today's classrooms, teachers are responsible for a lot, and I acknowledge that calling for attention to cheating adds to the growing list. However, we also know that the problem of cheating is only increasing, that virtually nothing is being done currently about the problem (and students know that, too), and that students often lack explicit exposure to concepts related to academic integrity. Making the required commitment requires five components.

First, as educators, we must learn about cheating, its causes, how students cheat, and appropriate ways of responding. Hopefully, Chapters 1 through 4 of this book have provided a good foundation. Other books, videotapes, organizations, and resources are available (see Resource C), and educators can take advantage of these.

Second, teachers must talk about cheating and provide instruction to their students about why cheating is wrong and about what constitutes honest and appropriate behavior on tests and written assignments. The status quo is that students are often not exposed by their teachers to exhortation about academic integrity or to instruction about how to avoid cheating. The same situation exists in students' homes. A subsequent *Who's Who* survey reported that over one third (34%) of the high school students questioned hadn't heard anything from their parents about cheating. According to Joe Krouse, associate publisher of the survey results,

> With such a casual attitude toward cheating on the part of so many parents and school authorities, it's no wonder more than half of the cheaters just shrug it off, saying "'it didn't seem like a big deal,'" said Krouse. "If the folks in charge of moral guidance don't make a bigger fuss about ethical behavior, it won't be a big deal." (Who's Who Among American High School Students, 1998, p. 1)

Third, teachers have opportunities to make small but important changes in their classroom tests, written assessments, and grading policies—changes that can have a big impact on the level of academic integrity in the classroom. Some recommended changes are described in detail in Chapter 5, and other sources are referenced there to help educators to improve these important elements of professional practice. Some simple mechanical changes can make cheating on tests and plagiarism less likely. At the systemic level, schools and districts can develop and implement policies on academic integrity (see Resource D) and teachers can help communicate these to students, parents, and others. However, perhaps the primary educational change involves the daily work by educators of fostering a learning orientation among students.

Fourth, we must be willing to act. According to one of the *Who's Who* (1996) surveys, 94% of high school students who said that they had cheated also reported that they were not caught. Of the small number who were caught cheating, 83% said that they received no punishment.

These facts are not without a larger consequence. For example, researchers have found that whether or not a student reported having cheated in college was significantly related to also reporting having seen other students cheat and to the student's impression of the percentage of other students who cheated (Bunn, Caudill, & Gropper, 1992). Other researchers have found that the best predictors of whether a student cheated were (1) observing others who cheat; (2) knowing other students who cheat; and (3) a student's perception of the degree of cheating that occurs (Mixon & Mixon, 1996). Witnessing the cheating of other students go unpunished is also a powerful factor in predicting whether a student will cheat; according to one of the earliest studies of this factor, one of the two major reasons that students said they cheated was that they had seen others get away with it (Ludeman, 1938). More recently, Heisler (1974) demonstrated that students cheat significantly less if they have witnessed another person being caught cheating.

Thus, responding to cheating is effective not only for guarding the validity of inferences based on assessments and for the benefit of the individual student involved; it has a much broader influence. Responding to even a single incident of cheating can help affirm the value and importance of honest behavior in other students' minds and help dissuade them from engaging in cheating themselves.

Finally, we must remember that, as teachers, we are unavoidably profound role models for our students. The problem of educators cheating on tests has been alluded to only briefly in this book, but there exists a potential for a powerful influence for better or worse in the way teachers approach student assessment. Only a handful of educators cheat; those who do harm the credibility of their colleagues who act with integrity, and teach the wrong lesson to their students. The majority who do not cheat are models also. The daily manner in which they approach the range of ethical issues in the classroom and model high standards of personal conduct can teach citizenship in ways that are more efficacious than any character curriculum. More important, they can make lasting differences in the lives of their students on the objectives of education that are not assessed by any test or term paper, and that are arguably the most important outcomes of all.

Resource A
Glossary

Ability test: A procedure designed to measure *potential* for achievement. Sometimes also referred to as *aptitude* tests. Nearly all ability tests used in classrooms are of the standardized, commercially produced variety, such as the *Otis-Lennon School Abilities Test* and the *Cognitive Abilities Test,* which can be used in conjunction with an achievement test to derive ability/achievement comparisons that describe the extent to which a student is "underachieving" or "overachieving" in school, given his or her measured potential. Another common use of ability tests such as the *Wechsler Intelligence Scale for Children—Revised* (WISC-R) is to identify students for placement in certain programs (e.g., special education, gifted education).

Achievement test: A procedure designed to measure a student's attainment of knowledge, skill, or ability. Examples of achievement tests include spelling tests, chemistry lab reports, oral questioning in class, and so on. Standardized achievement tests include the *Iowa Tests of Basic Skills,* the *Stanford Achievement Test,* and others.

Assessment: The process of gathering and synthesizing multiple sources of information for the purpose of describing or making decisions about a student. The term *assessment* has been borrowed from fields such as medicine and counseling, in which a patient or client may be given a variety of tests, the results of which must be synthesized—that is, analyzed and interpreted—by a single professional or team of experts. In education, assessment pertains most accurately to contexts such as special education, in which an Individualized Education Program (IEP) is planned for a student based on a variety of sources of information about the student. (Note: The term *assessment* is—incorrectly, though increasingly—used simply as a synonym for a test or assignment.)

Battery: A collection of tests. For example, the *Iowa Tests of Basic Skills* (ITBS) is one of several large-scale testing programs that offer what is called a *Complete Battery.* The group of individual tests in language, mathematics, study skills, and so on that are included in the ITBS constitutes an achievement battery.

Cheating: Any action that violates the established rules governing the administration of a test or completion of an assignment; any behavior that gives one student an unfair advantage over other students on a test or assignment; or any action that decreases the accuracy of the intended inferences arising from a student's performance on a test or assignment.

Content standards: Statements that describe specific knowledge, skills, or abilities over which students are expected to have mastery for a given age/grade and subject area.

Crib sheet: A piece of paper or other material on which inappropriate or unauthorized material is written for use during a test. Also known as a *cheat sheet.*

Criterion-referenced test (CRT): An instrument whose primary purpose is to gauge whether a student knows or can do specific things. CRTs may be developed and used in informal ways for classroom use, or may be instituted on a larger scale. In either case, the content of the test would be highly specific, the test would be tightly linked to specific objectives, and a criterion for judging success on the test would be specified a priori. Some examples of CRTs include weekly spelling tests, driver's license tests, vocational performance tests, and so forth, with the key characteristic of such tests being the presence of the specific criteria.

The simplest illustration of a CRT is the road portion of a driver's license test. In the parallel parking portion, the candidate for a license must meet certain *criteria:* for example, park the car within a marked area, in four minutes or less, without knocking over more than one orange pylon. A person's success or failure—manifested in whether or not the person gets a driver's license—does not depend on how well other candidates perform. In theory, all drivers could pass or all could fail. There is no distinction between one candidate who parks the vehicle perfectly in the middle of the space, in only two minutes, with no pylons knocked over, and the candidate who parks awkwardly within the space, in just under four minutes, and knocks one pylon over. Both candidates have met the criteria.

Evaluation: The process of ascribing value or worth to a score or performance. For example, a student may earn 40 out of 50 points on a term paper. Evaluation only takes place, however, when some judgment accompanies the score. The most common form of judgment is the assigning of grades. In this case, awarding a B to students who scored 40 out of 50 would be evaluation.

High stakes: The terms *high stakes* and *low stakes* refer to the severity of the consequences associated with performance on a test or assignment. For example, if a test is used to determine whether a high school student can graduate, the consequences of passing or failing it are obviously serious, and the test would be considered high stakes. On the other hand, weekly observations made by an elementary school teacher regarding her students' participation in class may be verbally communicated to parents during a parent-teacher conference, or may even count toward a student's "Effort" grade, but serious consequences or decisions about a student would not ordinarily follow. Such an evaluation would be termed "low stakes."

Honor code: A formal statement concerning the rights and responsibilities of students and teachers in academic settings, and the penalties for failing to uphold those responsibilities. The statement may be limited to matters of academic integrity, but may also deal with honesty, respect, and citizenship in the academic community more broadly. In settings where an honor code is in place, to be admitted to and remain in the academic community, participants must pledge to uphold the code and to report violations.

Item: A question on a test or assignment. If the question is written in the multiple-choice format, the item has a *stem* (the part that introduces the question) and several *options,* usually labeled A, B, C, D, and E or similarly. If the question asks the student to engage in a performance or demonstrate a skill such as writing an essay, the item consists of a *prompt* (the written or other material introducing the task) and a related scoring guide or *rubric.*

Item format: The style in which an item is constructed. Item formats are classified as either *select-response,* in which the student chooses the correct answer from alternatives provided (e.g., multiple-choice, matching, true/false), or *constructed-response* (sometimes also called *open-ended* or *supply-type*), in which an answer must be created by the student (e.g., essay, short-answer, speech, project, etc.).

Norm-referenced test (NRT): An instrument whose primary purpose is to describe the relative standing of students at a particular grade level. NRTs provide information about how a student's performance compares with a reference group of students, called the *norm group.* Familiar examples of NRTs include the *Iowa Tests of Basic Skills* (ITBS), the *Stanford Achievement Test, Ninth Edition* (SAT-9), the *Law School Admissions Test* (LSAT), and the *Graduate Record Examinations* (GRE).

Performance standards: Prescribed levels of performance representing differential degrees of knowledge, skill, or ability with respect to some content standards. Performance standards are often thought of as "cut scores" and are based on the number of points obtained on a task, the number of questions answered correctly on a test, and so forth. However, the descriptions of performance standards such as *Basic, Proficient,* and *Advanced* are most accurately thought of as the performance standards, while any cut scores are merely an operationalization of the performance standards in a particular context.

Plagiarism: Representing, in written or oral expression, the words, thoughts, or ideas of another without appropriate citation or referencing, usually for the purpose of intentionally misrepresenting such words, thoughts, or ideas as one's own.

Razoring: The removal of material from a source for the purpose of preventing others from gaining access to the source. The term comes from the use of a razor blade to excise pages from, for example, a book or journal held in a library reserve section. One student who wishes to gain an advantage over other students can cut out relevant pages from the reference material, then remove or destroy the material after using it for his or her work.

Reliability: The characteristic of being dependable. Because an assignment or test consists only of a sample of questions or tasks and because both the students who respond and those who score the responses are susceptible to various unpredictabilities in their performance (called *random errors*), no score can be considered a perfectly dependable snapshot of a student's performance. Various methods can be used to quantify the degree of confidence that can be placed in students' scores. All of the methods result in a number, called a *reliability coefficient,* that can take on any value from zero (0.0) to one (1.0). A reliability coefficient of 0.0 would denote completely undependable scores—no more useful for making decisions about students than flipping a coin or guessing. A reliability coefficient of 1.0 indicates perfect dependability (the complete absence of those pesky errors mentioned above) and the potential for the test scores to be used with great confidence for decision making. Values between 0.0 and 1.0 indicate relative poorer (nearer to 0.0) or greater (nearer to 1.0) dependability.

Rubric: A framework for scoring a performance, observation, essay, or other student-constructed response to an item or task. Also known as *scoring guides,* rubrics usually include a list of several elements along with sets of specific criteria for awarding points to the performance on each of the elements.

Standardized: Any uniform system of gathering information that is developed, administered, and scored under controlled conditions. Note, however, that the term *standardized* is unrelated to format. Although the multiple-choice format comes to mind when thinking of a standardized test, such tests can (and are) developed using any format (multiple-choice, true/false, performance tasks, oral, essay).

Standards-referenced test (SRT): Standards-referenced tests (SRTs) are similar to CRTs in that both attempt to describe the knowledge, skill, or abilities that students possess. Whereas CRTs express standards in terms of quantity and category (e.g., a percentage correct and passing/failing), SRTs link students' scores to concrete statements about what performance at the various levels means. Typically, SRTs are constructed to match *content standards,* and the SRT consists of a set of items or tasks constructed to measure the expected knowledge and skills. *Performance standards* are then established that describe how well students must perform in order to be classified as meeting a particular level of performance. State-mandated student testing for students in Grades K-12 for English Language Arts, Mathematics, and so on, would typically be considered to be SRTs to the extent that the tests are aligned with the state's content standards in those subjects.

Test: Any systematic sampling of a student's knowledge, skill, or ability. Ideally, those interested in a student's achievement would like to know everything about what the student can do. Because of time, cost, or other considerations they must usually settle for a subset of observations. However, to gather as many observations as practical, multiple sources of information are preferred, and tests or assignments are usually constructed to contain many questions, tasks, essays, and so on, or some combination of these.

Test form: A version of a test that can be used interchangeably with other versions. Because a test may be needed on more than one occasion, several versions of the test are usually developed. For example, the SAT is administered several times each year, though a different form is used each time. The items on each form are different, although there is no advantage to the student regardless of when the test is taken because the versions—or *forms*—are designed and analyzed in such a way as to yield comparable results.

Validity: The degree to which the conclusions yielded by any sample of behavior (e.g., a test, assignment, quiz, term paper, observation, interview, etc.) are meaningful, accurate, and useful. Validity is the degree to which a student's performance results in decisions about the student that are "correct," or inferences about the student's knowledge, skill, or ability that are "on target."

Resource B

Resources Used to Cheat

Sources for Term Papers

Some Web sites offer papers for free; others sell papers; some offer papers to those who pay an annual subscription fee; some allow students to download papers in exchange for submitting a paper. Nearly all of them have a silly disclaimer that warns users not to actually turn in the papers for assignments. Right.

I haven't counted, but I'd estimate that there are approximately 500 such sites altogether. The following entries provide an annotated sampling of some of what can be found on the Internet.

1. A to Z Term Papers (www.a-ztermpapers.com/)

This site presents the visitor with the usual hype: "Never struggle with writer's block or impossible research topics again! Get the help you need to ensure your success in any class. Our highly qualified academic professionals are available 24 hours a day to assist you with the research and examples you need to write a great term paper. Best of all, you don't have to waste hours in the library . . . "

Unlike other sites, however, A to Z claims that it does not sell prewritten papers, but custom writes each and every paper to the requested specifications. According to the site, "You don't get recycled term papers here; you get a paper written specifically for you, tailored to fit your needs. We write the paper you want, the way you want it."

Prices for papers are not listed, because "pricing is determined on a case-by-case basis, depending on the complexity of your paper." Users are "supplied with a full list of citations for all the material used."

The site contains a nice disclaimer—"All material . . . is intended for the sole purpose of research and exemplary purposes only. We encourage you to use our papers as a research and study aid only. Plagiarism is a crime, and we do not condone such behavior. Please use our material responsibly . . . "—though it is strangely reminiscent of beer makers' advertisements urging people to drink responsibly.

2. CheatHouse (www.cheathouse.com)

According to the home page, "CheatHouse is the perfect site for research, late assignments and general reference." The site is said to contain "thousands of essays in over 130 categories" and it claims to have been "leading the industry since 1995" with "over 5.5 million visitors served." Sounds like McDonald's.

3. Essay Boy (www.essayboy.com)

This site boasts an inventory of 25,000 papers for sale at $9.95 per page (bibliography pages are free). Each of the stock papers is available in English, German, Spanish, French, Italian, and Portuguese (although, for papers written in languages other than English, the site sends a free "backup" copy in English because "the translations are often a bit 'rough' around the edges." If a standard paper doesn't suit the user's needs, papers written to requested specifications are available at $19.95 per page.

4. Essay Crawler (www.essaycrawler.com)

This site has the usual term papers warehoused (according to the home page, 69,000 of them). However, the site also provides users with a "crawler" function. This feature allows the user to "search over 100,000 free essays with our metacrawler that search[es] 11 popular sites, or check out our 1000's of local essays and other exciting features! We are the MetaCrawler of the essay world, your portal site for free essays, term papers, and book reports. This engine searches purely free essay sites that house thousands of papers, so you can get done and get on with your life."

Another feature of this site allows the user to link to the "Top 25," "Top 50," or "Top 100" term paper sites.

Naturally, this site advertises itself only as an "additional resource." According to the site, they "do not recommend turning in the essays found via this website. Doing so would be plagiarism and could result in a 'zero,' or worse, especially if you signed a [sic] honor statement prior to enrollment. Use the essays and term papers on this site to give you ideas for your paper."

5. Essay Heaven (www.essayheaven.com)

This site advertises itself as the student's "guardian angel who knows how to write." The site claims to have an inventory of 35,000 critical, academic essays with immediate availability. To find salvation, "simply type in a keyword pertaining to your topic and easily enter the database of EssayHeaven.com and see what's available behind its pearly gates."

6. Essay Mill (www.essaymill.com)

I don't know if there is any way to verify Essay Mill's claim to be "the biggest essay database" on the Internet. The number of essays said to be available (170,000) is the largest inventory I have seen advertised. The majority of the 170,000 are available for purchase; about 2,000 are available without charge.

7. FastPapers (www.fastpapers.com/)

This site guarantees that "you WILL find a model research paper on THIS site or we'll write one as FAST as you need! There are more than 20,000 example term papers listed at Fastpapers.com—available for same-day delivery via email, fax or Federal Express!" The site also boasts that "all research is current and fully cited," that "all students pay one low rate," and that "all bibliography pages are absolutely FREE!" Of course, only the bibliography is free. The reports cost $9.95 per page, although the user is assured that "all papers are filled with 225 words per page!"

8. Genius Papers (www.geniuspapers.com)

This site doesn't say it provides papers, but calls itself a "research company." This is not its only distinction, however. The site is an example of a subscription service. Instead of paying by the page or by the paper, users pay a single annual subscription fee for unlimited access to the papers available at the site. According to the site,

> For over 6 years, Genius Papers has been one of the biggest and most comprehensive research companies on the Web. . . . Genius Papers has developed the premier set of services for students to have completed papers within a fraction of the time they are used to. We provide a database of thousands upon thousands of term papers, book reports, and essays. But that is where most research and term paper companies stop. We are just beginning. With your one-time $19.95 access fee, you will also receive a membership for the Genius Papers Academic Research Center.

9. Grade "A" Notes (www.gradeanotes.com/)

This site is actually a legitimate printer, publisher, and course pack producer. However, they provide a service that is susceptible to corruption and, according to some sources, represents a new generation of illegitimate term papers. For a fee, students can download from the site a complete set of course notes that can easily be turned into a model term paper. For example, the catalog offers notes recorded from the introductory psychology lectures of an Instructor Behling from the University of Michigan in the winter of 1999. According to the Web site, "This is an entire set of lecture notes taken by an experienced notetaker and provided in typed format. These notes are proven 'best-sellers.'"

10. History Papers (www.historypapers.net/)

Apparently, the term paper industry is becoming specialized, as this site is devoted exclusively to history term papers. So specialized, in fact, that the site boasts of being a "certified TPS help site." The site also lists some sister sites: The-Civil-War.com, Vietnam-War-Papers.com, and Russian-History.com.

The site offers the usual off-the-rack papers and custom tailoring services. Topic choices include U.S. history (colonial, 18th century, 19th century, and 20th century and beyond) and European history (pre-1700s, modern Europe, and Russia).

I had no idea how great the proliferation of term paper sites had become until I visited the "Links" section of the History Papers Web site. That page lists 133 different sites, including highly specialized sites such as those devoted exclusively to term papers about nursing, Gilgamesh, and Willy Loman (of Arthur Miller's *Death of a Salesman.*

11. Lazy Students (www.lazystudents.com)

Finally, I thought I had at least encountered some truth in advertising. But no. This site should get an award for the sheer chutzpa of its "blame the victim" advertising. According to the site, *teachers* are the reason that plagiarism exists. The site proclaims that "Term Papers Promote Laziness Among College Students" and that "writing term papers and research papers is the number one cause of laziness among college students." Under that logic, it actually makes sense to reason that, "If your professor can have a research assistant, why can't you?" The teacher made me cheat.

It would seem that with such an airtight case for the sale of term papers, the site would engage in commerce unabashedly. Ironically, though, the site warns the user:

"You probably think LazyStudents.com is one of those term paper mills that will write your term papers for you. If that is what you are looking for, LazyStudents.com may not be the right web site for you. We are different because we discourage plagiarism and do not have term paper writers working for us. Instead, we offer The Ultimate Student Hyperlist with access to over 50,000 sample term papers, research papers, theses, dissertation and research resources that will help you come up with quality term paper topics and research paper ideas. Don't be lazy, click here to join."

Is it just me or does the slogan "don't be lazy, download one of our term papers" make sense to anyone? Maybe I should download one of their Logic 101 papers to help me straighten this out.

12. Paper Geeks (www.papergeeks.com)

The home page for this site would have you believe that they are the most scholarly of the term paper mills. According to the site,

> We have no social life. Let's be frank! All we do is write research papers! We create research papers! We sell research papers! Since 1994 . . . our paper geeks have written more than 25,000 research papers! We're the biggest paper geeks on the internet! A group of knowledgeable, modest geniuses writing papers around the clock while everyone else has fun!!

Well, I may not be a paper geek, but I can do the math. Take 25,000 papers running about 7 pages each—that's 175,000 pages. Multiplying by $9.95 per page equals $1,741,250 . . . and that's if they sell each paper only once! Rich geeks.

13. Papers Online (www.papers-online.com/)

Sponsored by an organization called Collegiate Care Research Assistance, this site advertises "over 3,000 current term papers, reports, and essays." Users can "find any report you need quickly and easily" and "all essays are immediately downloadable!" If one of the "thousands of model term papers" ready for download isn't sufficient, Papers Online offers custom writing services. "Our writers are well trained and cover almost every topic and subject! Just tell us what you need and we'll deliver it fast and right the first time." And the company offers an online editing service. According to the site, "If you need a term paper or college admission essay edited, our professional writing staff can help! One of our experts will edit your report or essay for grammar, spelling, context and flow. We don't just tell you what's wrong, we make the changes and send you the final document!"

If some of the advertising sounds like Papers Online is trying to sell you a term paper, well, you must be mistaken. Like many sites, this one contains the usual perfunctory disclaimer: "IMPORTANT . . . PLEASE READ THIS! These reports are intended for RESEARCH PURPOSES ONLY, and we rely on your assurance that the following legal requirements will be followed: They may not be submitted either in whole or substantial part under any student's name in fulfillment of the requirements for a degree, diploma, certificate, or course of study at any postsecondary institution."

So much for the fine print. For fast service, users can also call 1-800-44-REPORT 24 hours a day, seven days a week. Visa, MasterCard, American Express, Discover, checks, and money orders are accepted. And, speaking of fine print, at $5.95 per page, I think I'll take mine in a tiny font, small margins, please.

14. School Sucks (www.schoolsucks.com)

This is probably the oldest and most notorious of the cheating resource sites. The site promises to "Download Your Workload" and offers free homework and term papers in 110 languages and 63 categories that can be identified by keyword or title search.

15. Term Paper Sites (www.termpapersites.com)

This site doesn't deal in term papers directly, but it is one of many such sites that provide an annotated listing of dozens of other sites that do. One-stop shopping.

Miscellaneous

The following items are not all necessarily useful for helping students to cheat, but they are all interesting resources for those who would like to know more about the topic.

1. *The Cheater's Handbook: The Naughty Student's Bible* (book). Corbett, B. (1999). New York: Regan Books.

This book is rarely carried in public libraries—especially those affiliated with schools, colleges, or universities—but is usually a hot item at other points of sale. When I checked for the book on Amazon.com, it urged me to "order soon" as only two copies were left in stock . . . but more were on the way.

2. *Spies Like Us* (DVD/VHS movie)

This Warner Brothers production is nearly universally acclaimed as a genuine B movie, starring Chevy Chase and Dan Aykroyd. Chase and Aykroyd play a pair of ne'er-do-well CIA desk jockeys who get the "opportunity" to engage in dangerous fieldwork after they are caught cheating on the foreign service board exam. Though not much of the movie is about cheating, there is a several-minute scene showing Chevy Chase engaging in every stereotypical cheating activity during the foreign service exam in his characteristic slapstick way. The movie doesn't glamorize cheating (Chase is caught and punished for the cheating), but it doesn't moralize against it, either. From a cinematic perspective, the movie is pretty bad, but you could certainly spend $2.99 at Blockbuster to get worse.

Resource C
Resources to Help Deter Cheating

Organizations Promoting Academic Integrity

There are several organizations whose primary mission is to promote academic integrity in educational settings and ethical behavior by those who work in those settings. The following information provides a brief overview of some of the resources available from these organizations.

The Center for Academic Integrity

As stated on its Web site, "The Center for Academic Integrity provides a forum to identify, affirm, and promote the values of academic integrity among students."

According to the site, the CAI offers the following:

- Resources for institutions and individuals who wish to begin a program emphasizing academic integrity
- Examples of honor codes in place at various institutions
- Specialized materials and information for high school and college levels
- An annual fall conference highlighting new research and practices related to academic integrity
- Links to other organizations involved in promoting academic integrity

Among the publications of the CAI is a booklet titled *The Fundamental Value of Academic Integrity*, single copies of which are available free upon request from the Center.

Contact information:

Center for Academic Integrity
Box 90434

Duke University
Durham, NC 27708

Tel: (919) 660-3045

Email: integrity@duke.edu

Internet: www.academicintegrity.org

The Josephson Institute

According to the home page for the Josephson Institute, "The Joseph and Edna Josephson Institute of Ethics is a public-benefit, non-partisan, nonprofit membership organization [with a mission] to improve the ethical quality of society by advocating principled reasoning and ethical decision making." Among other activities, the Institute sponsors a project called "Character Counts!" that promotes the values of trustworthiness, respect, responsibility, fairness, caring, and citizenship in the workplace, school, sports, and civic life. The Character Counts! project has a separate Web site found at www.character counts.org.

The Character Counts! site has a wealth of resources for K-12 teachers, including the following:

- Sample lesson plans that help teachers incorporate character lessons
- Inspirational essays by prominent Americans
- A tutorial that provides comprehensive background information for teachers on ethics, values, and decision-making models
- Results from the annual "Survey on Youth Violence and Substance Abuse"
- Links to and reviews of recent articles and books on character in the classroom, workplace, and athletics

Contact information:

The Joseph and Edna Josephson Institute of Ethics
4640 Admiralty Way, Suite 1001
Marina del Rey, CA 90292-6610

Tel: (310) 306-1868

Internet: www.josephsoninstitute.org

Center for the Fourth and Fifth Rs

In addition to the three R's of Reading, 'Riting, and 'Rithmetic, schools interested in addressing academic integrity should also devote energy to developing the characteristics of Respect and Responsibility. According to their Web site, the Center for the Fourth and Fifth Rs "disseminates articles on character education, sponsors an annual summer institute in character education, publishes a Fourth and Fifth Rs newsletter, and is building a network of 'Fourth and Fifth Rs Schools' committed to teaching respect, responsibility and other core virtues as the basis of good character."

Besides information on the Center's efforts, the Web site also contains descriptions and links to other organizations involved in character and ethical education, as well as lists of books, videos, and other resources on those topics.

Contact information:

Center for the Fourth and Fifth Rs
State University of New York at Cortland
P.O. Box 2000
Cortland, NY 13045

Tel: (607) 753-2455

Email: c4n5rs@cortland.edu

Internet: www.cortland.edu/www/c4n5rs/

Books on Cheating and Plagiarism

Many books (and articles) have been written on the topics of cheating, plagiarism, and academic integrity. The following list provides a sampling (in alphabetical order by author) of some of the resources most directly relevant or of interest to educators in K-12 settings.

1. Cizek, G. J. (1999). *Cheating on Tests: How to Do It, Detect It, and Prevent It*. Mahwah, NJ: Lawrence Erlbaum.

This book is focused mainly on cheating on tests (i.e., it doesn't address plagiarism), and it tries to take a scholarly approach but in such a way as to make the book accessible to a wide audience. It covers every aspect of cheating on tests in a good depth.

2. Lathrop, A., & Foss, K. (2000). *Student Cheating and Plagiarism in the Internet Era.* Englewood, CO: Libraries Unlimited.

This book is focused mainly on plagiarism, with specific emphasis on how students use electronic resources to cheat. It takes a pragmatic approach to the problem and includes many resources that educators can copy and use in the classroom.

3. Mallon, T. (1989). *Stolen Words.* New York: Ticknor and Fields.

This is a classic, scholarly work on plagiarism. It is not likely to be practically useful for teachers, but provides the most authoritative, engaging, and witty background on the origins and contemporary examination of the issue.

4. Whitley, B. E., Jr., & Keith-Spiegel, P. (2002). *Academic Dishonesty: An Educator's Guide.* Mahwah, NJ: Lawrence Erlbaum.

This book was written by two specialists in the area of ethics in higher education. It focuses on helping college and university personnel understand and address cheating at the postsecondary level, but much of their advice can be adapted for use in precollegiate settings.

Software for Detecting Cheating and Plagiarism

For the educator who is interested in using technology to address cheating, a wide variety of software and Web-based detecting technology can be purchased or obtained for free. The list below (ordered alphabetically) is highly variable in terms of quality, price, and method. However, it should give the user a good idea of the range of what is available and what capabilities exist.

1. CopyCatch

www.copycatch.freeserve.co.uk/vocalyse.htm

This United Kingdom site offers a text analysis program called "CopyCatch" for sale. According to the site, the software was "written by a forensic linguist with extensive experience in the detection of plagiarism and collusion." The software examines the degree of similarity between text materials submitted by a class of students and flags pairs of text using an instructor-defined criterion. Flags are assigned to pairs of writing samples that exhibit either unusually high similarity (which the software developers state may suggest plagiarism) or unusually low similarity (which they say may indicate "highly original thinking or an obtained essay"). An IBM-compatible version of CopyCatch costs £250 (about $365).

2. Essay Verification Engine

www.canexus.com/eve/

(See also the more extensive description of this cheating detection software in Chapter 4.)

This Essay Verification Engine software, version 2.0 (EVE2), is software that users purchase to install on a local computer for subsequent local analysis of written text for potential plagiarism. The software takes as input electronic samples of student writing in various formats (plain text, Microsoft Word, or WordPerfect) and compares the writing to material available on the Internet. Output consists of links to Web pages a student may have plagiarized, a statistic to estimate the total percentage of the essay plagiarized, and an annotated copy of the student's essay with suspected plagiarized portions highlighted. A free 15-day trial version of the software can be downloaded. The software can be purchased for $19.99 per licensee (i.e., per teacher).

3. Glatt Plagiarism Services, Inc.

www.plagiarism.com

(See also the more extensive description of this cheating detection software in Chapter 4.)

This vendor offers a complete plagiarism program consisting of three components. The Glatt Plagiarism Teaching Program (GPTeach) is a computer-based tutorial for students intended to familiarize them with what constitutes plagiarism and how to avoid it. The program includes an instructional component on definitions of plagiarism, instruction on when and how to provide attribution, practice rewriting exercises, and mastery tests of key concepts.

The second component of the system is the Glatt Plagiarism Screening Program (GPSP) that, according to the site, is "a highly sophisticated screening program to detect plagiarism; typically used in academic institutions or in the legal profession for cases of copyright infringement."

The final component is called the Glatt Plagiarism Self-Detection Program (GPSD), which is essentially a less sophisticated version of the GPSP that permits users (including students) to evaluate the possibility of plagiarism in their written work.

4. Global Academic Integrity Service

www.plagiserve.com

The plagiarism detection analysis available from Global Academic Integrity Service is called "PlagiServe." The system analyzes written text, searches an in-house database of 250,000 student papers and Internet documents for potential sources of the text, and provides a summary index of document originality that is referred to as a "percentage of improper referencing." According to the Web site, an instructor who submits papers electronically from a class of students can be "absolutely confident that the papers . . . will be processed by Document Originality Module in less than 12 hours."

PlagiServe is one component of the company's umbrella service called "EduTie." An institution can purchase the EduTie system to facilitate online student paper submission and processing, originality detection, electronic grading, and archiving of documents.

5. Plagiarism.org

www.turnitin.com or www.plagiarism.org

(See also the more extensive description of this cheating detection software in Chapter 4.)

The two sites listed are companion sites; either of these links will get you to a source for plagiarism detection software and a writing instruction tutorial designed to serve as an aid in helping students develop writing skills and avoid plagiarism. Free registration provides interested users with a complementary 30-day trial of the system.

6. Plagiarism Sleuth

www.2learn.ca/mapset/SafetyNet/plagiarism/sleuth/StringSearch new.html

The above link is to a crude plagiarism detection tool that is part of a larger Web site devoted to academic integrity. To use the site, a teacher types a small amount of text from a suspect student paper and a search is performed in an attempt to match the text to various Internet sources. This is accomplished via the user selecting a search engine (e.g., Google, Lycos, Yahoo) from a pull-down menu. Basically, this system is just a different interface for the kind of search a user would do who was more familiar with search engines. The real value of this tool lies in the introduction to search logic and practice search activities accompanying the tool and found at other links on the site:

www.2learn.ca/research/search.html and

www.2learn.ca/mapset/SafetyNet/plagiarism/plagactivity1.html

7. *Scrutiny!*

www.assess.com (Assessment Systems Corporation)

(See also the more extensive description of this cheating detection software in Chapter 4.)

Scrutiny! is the only fully supported, commercially available software for detecting copying on multiple-choice tests. The software is available in a Windows version for installation and use on a local personal computer. It comes with easy-to-follow instructions and can be used with test data from classes of typical size (i.e., approximately 25 students). The suggested price for *Scrutiny!* is $399.00, or $299.00 for educational institutions. A free demonstration version is downloadable from the Web site listed above.

8. WCopyfind

http://plagiarism.phys.virginia.edu/Wsoftware.html

This software is available from the University of Virginia Plagiarism Resource Center and was prepared by a physics professor, Lou Bloomfield, of the University of Virginia. The software is freely downloadable, subject to only a few restrictions on its use. The program requires the user to specify electronic files (papers, writing samples, or passages of text) for comparison. It then analyzes the input to identify documents that share large amounts of text. The latest version of the program (v. 2.1a) has many user-definable criteria, including tools that allow the user to specify the following: shortest phrase to match; fewest matches to report; shortest text string to consider; minimum percentage of matching words; and switches to allow the user to ignore punctuation, ignore numbers, and ignore letter case.

9. WordCHECK DP

www.wordchecksystems.com

The WordCHECK DP software (where "DP" stands for "Document Profiling") is a Windows-based application for use on a local (i.e., classroom or school building) computer. The system analyzes similarities between pairs of text entries using a keyword analysis approach. To use the system, a teacher inputs student writing in the form of an electronic file. The software then analyzes the document and forms a keyword index for the document and a keyword library. The system also allows users to search for matching documents based upon keyword use and specific patterns.

The WordCHECK DP software can be purchased in two versions: Profiler Basic ($95 regular price/$59 educational institutions) or

WordCHECK DP Profiler Pro ($295 regular/$179 educational). A free (30 days) demonstration version of the program can be downloaded directly from the site at www.wordchecksystems.com/download. html

Web Sites Devoted to Academic Integrity/Cheating Prevention

Just as the number of Web sites devoted to cheating, term paper mills, and so on has proliferated, so too have Web sites with the primary mission of combating cheating and promoting academic integrity. There are too many to catalog in a brief resource such as this, but the following annotated list should provide K-12 educators with highly relevant and practical information. The Web sites are listed alphabetically and each of the following summaries includes a brief description of the site's most useful feature(s).

1. Academic Integrity at Princeton

www.princeton.edu/pr/pub/integrity/index.html

This site is typical of many university sites that define, defend, and promote academic integrity. Various links on the site point to the Princeton University Honor Code and sections that provide information about how and when to cite sources, proper and improper assistance, and so on. The site is listed here because of the noteworthy and concrete examples and non-examples of plagiarism that should be very helpful in instructing students. The direct link to that portion of the site is

http://www.princeton.edu/pr/pub/integrity/pages/plagiarism.html

2. Cheating: An Insider's Guide to Cheating at Lakeview High School

http://academic.kellogg.cc.mi.us/k12lincolnm/cheating98.pdf

This site has a model of a simple, straightforward, complete, and informative booklet for high school students. The above link is to a short (4 pages) Acrobat file consisting of a student handbook prepared by Margaret Lincoln, a library media specialist at Lakeview High School (Battle Creek, MI). The booklet's table of contents includes definitions and specific examples of cheating (and how to avoid it) and sections addressing "Why You Shouldn't Cheat," "How We Know You Cheat," "How You Get Caught," and "Consequences of Cheating." This is a model for what elementary and secondary schools can and should provide to students.

3. Cheating 101: Paper Mills and You

www.coastal.edu/library/papermil.htm

This Web site is essentially the contents of a 1999 teaching effec-tiveness seminar presented by faculty members Margaret Fain and Peggy Bates of Coastal Carolina University (Conway, SC). The site provides a good overview of the detection and prevention of plagia-rism. Though targeted to a university faculty audience, the informa-tion is presented in such a way as to be valuable to educators at all levels.

4. Electronic Plagiarism Seminar

www.lemoyne.edu/library/plagiarism.htm

The title pretty much says it all. The content of the site was developed by Gretchen Pearson, a librarian at LeMoyne College (Syracuse, NY). This site, too, is well suited to educators at all levels, and has abundant documentation and links to other resources. The site focuses exclusively on plagiarism; it has infor-mation on definitions, copyright, detecting and preventing plagia-rism, links to term paper mills and plagiarism detection sites, and extensive bibliographies.

5. Plagiarism

www.csubak.edu/ssric/Modules/Other/plagiarism.htm

This site consists of only a personal essay by Professor Earl Babbie, Department of Sociology, Chapman University (Orange, CA). The link to the essay is through the Social Sciences Research and Instructional Council at California State University—Bakersfield. The essay is short but is mentioned here because of its excellent examples and non-examples of plagiarism, demonstrated by showing a passage of text fol-lowed by several variations of paraphrasing and commentary regarding why the paraphrases constitute plagiarism. These are good examples of the kinds of concrete illustrations that can be used to teach students appropriate skills.

6. Plagiarism in Colleges in [the] USA

www.rbs2.com/plag.htm

This site was developed by a New Hampshire attorney, Ronald Standler. A brief portion of the site provides a definition of plagiarism and copyright, and gives some guidelines for avoiding plagiarism. The majority of the site is devoted to statutes and court decisions related to plagiarism and copyright law.

7. Plagiarism Q & A

http://www.ehhs.cmich.edu/~mspears/plagiarism.html

This site is one of the only (and best) sites on plagiarism specifically targeting high school students and teachers. The site was developed by a high school teacher, Michael L. Spears, a Spanish teacher at Grosse Pointe Hills North High School in Michigan. The site includes many useful portions for educators (definition of plagiarism; information on Spears's inservice program; review of typical penalties for plagiarism) and students (information on how to quote, summarize, or paraphrase; how to avoid plagiarizing; how to cite sources and create a bibliography; etc.).

8. Plagiarism: What It Is and How to Recognize and Avoid It

www.indiana.edu/~wts/wts/plagiarism.html

This site contains information on plagiarism developed by a Writing Tutorial Services unit at Indiana University (Bloomington, IN). Of particular note on this site are the several examples that teachers can use with students for teaching them how to recognize unacceptable and acceptable paraphrasing.

9. Thinking and Talking About Plagiarism

http://bedfordstmartins.com/technotes/techtiparchive/ttip102401.htm

This site is a page of "Tech Notes" presented by a book publisher (Bedford and St. Martin's Publishers). It provides a number of teaching tips for instructing students about plagiarism, suggestions for crafting writing assignments that are less susceptible to plagiarism, and links to other plagiarism information.

10. University of Virginia Plagiarism Resource Center

http://plagiarism.phys.virginia.edu/

A bare-bones site, devoted exclusively to plagiarism. The site has links to other sites dealing with plagiarism and offers free downloadable software to detect plagiarism for Windows-based and Linux operating systems. For a description of this product, see the entry "WCopyfind" in the Software section of this Resource.

Other Resources

The following two items resisted easy classification under the preceding headings. Both are excellent resources for teachers as well as students.

1. *Cheaters* (DVD/VHS movie)

This movie is an HBO production that dramatizes the real events of the Steinmetz (IL) high school Academic Decathlon team. In 1995, Steinmetz students participated in the Decathlon—an annual academic competition in which students from schools within a state vie to win their state events and, if successful, advance to a national competition. Steinmetz won the Illinois competition, but protests by another school that Steinmetz had cheated prompted an investigation. The allegations included that students had obtained advance copies of the questions to be used in the competition, and it was discovered that, during the 1995 competition, "a Steinmetz student apparently took the name tag of a judge in the speech contest, posed as the official, and awarded his highest score to a classmate" (Harp, 1995, p. 14). The movie can be ordered directly from the HBO site.

2. On-line Multimedia Plagiarism Tutorial

http://www.library.dal.ca/how/emodules/intro.htm

This online tutorial was produced by Fran Nowakowski, a reference librarian at Dalhousie University (Halifax, Nova Scotia, Canada). Students can pace themselves through images, examples, sound clips, and lessons to learn what plagiarism is, how to avoid it, and so on. Some of the information in the tutorial may not be relevant (e.g. how to use the reference resources at Dalhousie's Killam Library), but overall, this link should be very helpful for any secondary school student.

Note: High school composition teachers or others may want to include a link to this site in a syllabus, or assign independent completion of the tutorial to students in a class. The tutorial requires an Internet connection (faster is better), Netscape or Internet Explorer browsers (versions 3.0 or higher), and an installed plug-in for the browser called Macromedia Authorware Web Player, version 6.0. All but the latter are already likely to be available on a school-based computer or on the student's home computer. The Authorware Web Player is available as a free download at http://www.macromedia.com/software/authorware/download/

Resource D

Sample Cheating Policies and Honor Codes

Sample Guidelines for Students Regarding Cheating and Plagiarism

"How to Avoid Cheating and Plagiarism"

www.umanitoba.ca/student/resource/student_advocacy/cheating-plagiarism-fraud.shtml

In tests and exams:

1. Do not sit near friends.

2. Shield your answer sheet so that others cannot see it.

3. Take no notes, books or other items into a test or exam except those expressly authorized. If unsure about what is permitted, always ask.

4. Do not gaze around the room when writing a test or exam.

5. Do not communicate with any other student during a test or exam: communicate only with the instructor or proctor.

6. Arrive on time. Hand in all papers required.

7. If you hear of anyone obtaining information about a test or exam in advance, report it to the instructor without delay.

8. If procedures for administering or supervising tests or exams seem inadequate to you, let the instructor or other authority know what your concerns are.

9. Report to the invigilator or instructor any unusual or suspicious behavior of other students writing the test or exam.

In essays, reports and other assignments:

1. Know the rules, including the specific rules for the specific assignment.

2. Do not work with a fellow student on any assignment unless authorized to do so. It is called "inappropriate collaboration" if you exceed the amount of group work expected by the Professor. **Make sure you clearly understand the Professor's expectations for individual and group work on each assignment/project.**

3. Acknowledge all assistance received, including help from friends or others in terms of proofreading, suggestions or information.

4. Do not submit work that is not entirely yours i.e. use of another student's essay, use of a downloaded essay from the Net, use of an assignment purchased from a service/agency.

5. Do not cite in your bibliography any books, articles or other sources (e.g. including the World Wide Web) which you have not used for the assignment in question.

6. Do not lend your work to other students unless you feel certain they will not use it dishonestly.

7. Keep a photocopy of all assignments, essays, and reports you hand in to be graded. Keep rough copies and notes until your final grade is received. Notes and rough copies can constitute valuable evidence that your work is your own.

8. If you submit an assignment by sliding it under an instructor's office door (not recommended), confirm the next day or as soon as you can that the assignment was received. Make a note of the actual time and date of submission.

9. The assignment you prepare for one course *should not* be used for a different course. This is called "duplicate submission."

10. When in doubt about any practice, ask your instructor. Do not rely on friends, relatives or fellow students for information about what is acceptable academic practice in a particular course or discipline.

11. When material you read impresses you, be particularly careful to use your own words. Use quotation marks and cite sources whenever you use the words of another, even phrases *only one or two words in length*. Acknowledge all sources of information and inspiration.

Sample Cheating Policies

1. Huntington Middle School (San Marino, CA) Cheating Policy

http://henry.san-marino.k12.ca.us/~heh/Binderreminder/binder frame.html (click on "Discipline/Suspensions" link)

CHEATING POLICY
You are cheating if you:

- Copy, fax, or duplicate assignments that will each be turned in as original.
- Exchange assignments by print-out, disk transfer, or modem, then submit as original.
- Write formulas, codes, key words on your person or objects for use in a test.
- Use hidden reference sheets during a test.
- Use programmed material in watches or calculators, when prohibited.
- Exchange answers with others (either give or receive answers).
- Take someone else's assignment and submit it as your own.
- Submit material (written or designed by someone else) without giving the author/artist name and/or source.
- Take credit for group work, when little contribution was made.
- Do not follow additional specific guidelines on cheating as established by department, class, or a certain teacher.

In assignments where the teacher specifically assigns a pair or group of students to work together, group members may share information, but individual students still have the responsibility for their share of the work.

Students caught cheating will receive no credit on that assignment and their class citizenship grade will be lowered for the first offense. Subsequent offenses will be dealt with more severely, in cooperation with Administration. The school-wide citizenship grade will be lowered at least one grade and the parents will be called. Cheating offenses may result in a "D" or "F" in citizenship, suspension, removal from elected positions and honorary organizations, the inability to participate in school activities, and similar consequences.

2. University of Michigan, Department of English Plagiarism Policy

http://www.lsa.umich.edu/english/undergraduate/plag.htm

Plagiarism occurs when the student submitting a paper for a course:

1. Does not properly attribute words or ideas to a source. That is, even if you're not quoting directly from a book you've read on "Macbeth"—a book that's helped you formulate ideas for your paper—you should nevertheless footnote that book at the point in the text where that other author's ideas helped shape your own essay.

2. Quotes from another author's writing without citing that author's work. This, of course, includes failing to cite material you take from the World Wide Web, as well as copying material from library books or your peer's papers.

3. Cites, with quotation marks, portions of another author's work, but uses more of that work without quotation marks and without attribution.

4. Takes a paper, in whole or in part, from a site on the Web or a "library" of already-written papers.

5. Steals a paper from another student and then submits that paper as coursework.

6. Submits the same paper twice for two different assignments.

7. Takes the results of another's research and attempts to pass those results off as his or her own work. This includes "citing" material from sources that have been gathered by another author. You can, of course, cite materials that you have found in another published text, but you need to make it quite clear that you are availing yourself of another author's research: your citation should specify where you found the material, rather than simply giving that material's original source.

If you are caught plagiarizing, the Department's usual policy is as follows:

a. You will fail the assignment and the course.
b. Your case will be forwarded, with an explanatory letter and all pertinent materials, to the Dean of Student Affairs.
c. You will be placed on academic probation (which does register on your transcript). If a student already on probation is caught plagiarizing, he or she is usually asked to leave the University.

Please understand that, in the intellectual community of this University, plagiarism is a form of stealing: there are few more serious breaches of intellectual community.

3. Elgin (IL) Community College, Department of English Policy on Plagiarism

http://www.elgin.edu/geninfo/public/shared/eccplagiarism.html

Plagiarism is the presentation of another person's written words or ideas as one's own. Students are guilty of plagiarism if they submit as their own work:

- part or all of a written assignment copied from another person's manuscript or notes
- part or all of an assignment copied or paraphrased from a source, such as a book, magazine, pamphlet or electronic document, without giving proper documentation
- the sequence of ideas, arrangement of material, pattern or thought of someone else, even though you express it in your own words; plagiarism occurs when such a sequence of ideas is transferred from a source to a paper without processes of digestion, integration and reorganization in the writer's mind, and without acknowledgment in the paper.

Students are guilty of being accomplices to plagiarism if they:

- allow their paper, in outline or finished form, to be copied and submitted as the work of another
- prepare a written assignment for another student and allow it to be submitted as that student's own work
- keep or contribute to a file of papers with the clear intent that these papers will be copied or submitted as work of anyone other than the author; students who know their work is being copied are presumed to consent to its being copied.

At its worst, plagiarism is deliberate dishonesty, as is the case in copying work from a book or article and presenting it as one's own, or in the case of copying another student's work and presenting it as one's own. Such a blatant, deliberate act amounts to academic theft and is a highly serious offense within the college community. The English Department recommends that a student guilty of deliberate plagiarism receive an automatic grade of "F" for the entire course in which the plagiarism occurs.

Another kind of plagiarism may sometimes be the result of ignorance, fear or insecurity. This kind of plagiarism presents the words or ideas of other persons or writers without the proper quotation marks, documentation, acknowledgment or citation of the source. For example, all words copied from another source must always be placed in quotation marks and correctly documented by author and page. Failure to do so is a form of plagiarism.

Also, ideas and information which are not "common knowledge"— that is, broadly known to most high school graduates—must be documented by author and page. The English Department recommends that a student guilty of this type of plagiarism, whether intentional or out of ignorance, receive an "F" for the assignment in which the misrepresentation occurs.

Cases of plagiarism or suspected plagiarism will be handled between the student and the instructor of the course. Subsequent actions may include notification of the appropriate dean and/or the counseling service.

Sample Honor Codes

1. Duke University Undergraduate Honor Code

http://registrar.duke.edu/registrar/honor.htm

An essential feature of Duke University is its commitment to integrity and ethical conduct. Duke's honor system helps to build trust among students and faculty and to maintain an academic community in which a code of values is shared. Instilling a sense of honor, and of high principles that extend to all facets of life, is an inherent aspect of a liberal education.

As a student and citizen of the Duke University Community:

- I will not lie, cheat, or steal in my academic endeavors.
- I will forthrightly oppose each and every instance of academic dishonesty.
- I will communicate directly with any person or persons I believe to have been dishonest. Such communication may be oral or written. Written communication may be signed or anonymous.
- I will give prompt written notification to the appropriate faculty member and to the Dean of Trinity College or the Dean of the School of Engineering when I observe academic dishonesty in any course.
- I will let my conscience guide my decision about whether my written report will name the person or persons I believe to have committed a violation of this Code.

2. University of Virginia Honor System

http://www.virginia.edu/summer/application/honor.pdf

To Prospective Students:

Since 1842, the University of Virginia has benefited from a body of community ethical standards realized in the Honor System. It is based on the presupposition that the absence of lying, cheating, and stealing from the University community promotes an atmosphere of mutual trust conducive to the pursuit of a worthwhile education.

The history of the Honor System reveals that it is not a static or outdated tradition. It has undergone many changes since its foundation in 1842 to meet the needs and standards of each current body. Virginia students have upheld the System because of the type of community it generates and because of the positive effect living in such a community has on each student.

The University community enjoys an agreement among its members that they shall not tolerate lying, cheating, or stealing. Every student is expected by his peers to conduct himself honorably and is expected to leave if he will not do so. Students found guilty of an honor offense are without exception *dismissed permanently* from the University. By enrolling in the University, a student joins in that agreement as embodied in the Honor System.

The Honor System has generally been regarded as one of the University's most notable and respected traditions. But this System is more than revered tradition or lofty idea. It is an institution which has constantly been re-examined and re-affirmed, one which brings concrete benefits both to individual students and to the University as a whole. Students at Virginia can be proud to live in an academic environment where one's word is accepted without question by students, faculty and administrators alike; where one can take unproctored tests and leave an examination room for a breath of fresh air without the fear of suspicion; where local merchants will accept a check upon one's identity as a University student; and where one may leave his possessions unattended on the Grounds and return to find them undisturbed.

The student body has gained many privileges because of the trust placed in University students, and the community has thrived on this trust. It is up to every student to ensure that this trust is not abused. As the Honor System is entirely student administered, this is a responsibility which is not taken lightly.

Students are expected to uphold the community of trust by not lying, cheating or stealing, and are strongly encouraged to either confront a fellow student who has committed an honor offense, or initiate a case with the Honor Committee.

Every person who is considering attending the University should be aware of the Honor System and of the responsibilities its maintenance places on University students. The Honor Committee welcomes inquiries from interested persons concerning any aspect of the System.

I, the undersigned, have read the above explanation of the Honor System and I understand that as a student of the University I will be participating in this system. I agree to support and abide by the Honor System, which prohibits lying, cheating, and stealing. I understand and accept that the Honor System is administered entirely by student representatives, including investigations, adjudication and appeal review, and that violations will result in permanent expulsion and revocation of any University degree.

_____   _____
Date   Signature

3. Langley High School (Fairfax County, VA, Public Schools) Honor Code

www.fcps.k12.va.us/LangleyHS/saxon/honor.html

At Langley, we strive to create an environment wherein all act honestly. We believe it is the right, privilege, and responsibility of each individual to contribute to and work in an environment of trust.

Even though the following document refers to academic policy, honorable behavior covers the full range of activities within the school environment. **Infractions of a "non-academic nature" will fall under the guidelines of the *Student Responsibilities and Rights* handbook.**

The honor code of Langley High School addresses cheating, plagiarizing, lying, and stealing.

Cheating encompasses, but is not limited to, the following:

– Willful giving or receiving of an unauthorized, unfair, dishonest, or unscrupulous advantage in school work over other students.
– Attempted cheating.
– Some examples are: deception; the use of talking, signs, or gestures during a quiz; copying from another student or allowing the copying of an individual assignment; passing test or quiz information during a class period or from one class period to members of another class period with the same teacher; submission of pre-written writing assignment at times when such assignments are supposed to be written in class; illegally exceeding time limits on timed tests, quizzes, or assignments; unauthorized use of study aids, notes, books, data, or other information; computer fraud; sabotaging the projects or experiments of other students.

Plagiarizing encompasses, but is not limited to, the following:

– Presenting as one's own, the works or the opinions of someone else without proper acknowledgment.
– Borrowing of the sequence of ideas, the arrangement of materials, or the pattern of thought of someone else without proper acknowledgment.

– Some examples are: having a parent or another person write an essay or do a project which is then submitted as one's own work; failing to use proper documentation and bibliography.

Lying encompasses, but is not limited to, the following:

– Willful and knowledgeable telling of an untruth or falsehood as well as any form of deceit, attempted deception, or fraud in an oral or written statement.
– Some examples are: lying or failing to give complete information to a teacher; feigning illness to gain extra preparation time for tests, quizzes, or assignments due.

Stealing encompasses, but is not limited to, the following:

– Taking or appropriating without the right or permission to do so and with the intent to keep or make use of wrongfully, the school work or materials of another student or the instructional materials of a teacher.
– Some examples are: stealing copies of tests or quizzes, illegitimately accessing the teacher's answer key for tests or quizzes; stealing the teacher's edition of the textbook; stealing another student's homework, notes, or handouts.

RESPONSIBILITIES
Students will:

1. Avoid situations which might contribute to cheating, plagiarizing, lying, and stealing.

2. Avoid unauthorized assistance on all school work.

3. Document borrowed materials by citing sources.

4. Avoid plagiarizing by:
    a. using quotation marks for statements taken from others.
    b. acknowledging information, ideas, or patterns of thought borrowed from any source.
    c. consulting faculty about any questionable situations.

In addition, students are encouraged to speak to any student they observe violating the Honor Code about the seriousness of the infraction.

Parents will:

1. Have knowledge of the Langley High School Honor Code and its consequences.

2. Provide a positive example for adhering to the Honor Code.

3. Support faculty and administration in enforcing the Honor Code.

Teachers will:

1. Take immediate action when violations related to school are determined.
   a. Counsel the student.
   b. Record a zero for the assignment with no opportunity for make-up work.
   c. Report the violation to the student's counselor and administrator on a discipline referral form. Confer with the assistant principal if possible.
   d. Contact the student's parent. One suggested method: The teacher might tell the student to notify his/her parents and request that the parent call the teacher within 24 hours. If the teacher is not called, then the teacher calls the parents. This procedure puts the responsibility on the student to confront the parent; such confrontation may serve as a deterrent to further violations.

2. Structure conditions during testing to alleviate the possibility of cheating.

3. Specify the types of collaboration that are discouraged and those that are encouraged.

4. Teach or review correct use of documentation when assigning work.

5. Review the Honor Code during the first week of the school year. Teachers are encouraged to review periodically the Honor Code as it relates to a specific discipline.

Counselors will:

1. Maintain cumulative records of reported violations of the Honor Code.

2. Facilitate Honor Code violation conferences when follow-up counseling is deemed appropriate by the student, parent, teacher, counselor, or administrator.

Administrators will:

1. Assure that all faculty, students and parents have knowledge of the Langley High School Honor Code.

2. Create a school-wide environment which encourages adherence to the Honor Code.

3. Encourage teachers to enforce the Honor Code.

4. Maintain cumulative records of reported violations of the Honor Code.

5. Facilitate Honor Code violation conferences among the student/parent/teacher/counselor when follow-up action is appropriate.

6. Enforce appropriate disciplinary actions in accordance with the *Student Responsibilities and Rights* handbook guidelines.

References

Advanced Psychometrics Incorporated. (1993). *Scrutiny!* [computer software]. St. Paul, MN: Author.

Albas, D., & Albas, C. A. (1993). Disclaimer mannerisms of students: How to avoid being labeled as cheaters. *Canadian Review of Sociology & Anthropology, 30*(4), 451-467.

American Educational Research Association, American Psychological Association, National Council on Measurement in Education. (1999). *Standards for educational and psychological testing.* Washington, DC: American Educational Research Association.

Ames, G. A., & Eskridge, C. W. (1992). The impact of ethics courses on student attitudes and behavior regarding cheating. *Journal of College Student Development, 33*(6), 556-557.

Anderman, E. M., Griesinger, T., & Westerfield, G. (1998). Motivation and cheating during early adolescence. *Journal of Educational Psychology, 90*(1), 84-93.

Antion, D. L., & Michael, W. B. (1983). Short-term predictive validity of demographic, affective, personal and cognitive variables in relations to two criterion measures of cheating behaviors. *Educational and Psychological Measurement, 43*(2), 467-482.

Arter, J. A., & McTighe, J. (2001). *Scoring rubrics in the classroom: Using performance criteria for assessing and improving student performance.* Thousand Oaks, CA: Corwin Press.

Baird, J. S., Jr. (1980). Current trends in college cheating. *Psychology in the Schools, 17*(4), 515-522.

Baldwin, D. C., Daughtery, S. R., Rowley, B. D., & Schwarz, M. R. (1996). Cheating in medical school: A survey of second-year students at 31 schools. *Academic Medicine, 71*(3), 267-273.

Bates, P., & Fain, M. (2002). *Detecting plagiarized papers.* Available at http://www.coastal.edu/library/plagiarz.htm

Bellezza, F. S., & Bellezza, S. F. (1989). Detection of cheating on multiple-choice tests by using error similarity analysis. *The Teaching of Psychology, 16*(3), 151-155.

Bishop, J., Mane, F., Bishop, M., & Moriarty, J. (2000). *The role of end-of-course exams and minimum competency exams in standards-based reforms* (Working Paper 00-09). Ithaca, NY: Cornell University Center for Advanced Human Resource Studies.

Black, D. (1962). The falsification of reported examination marks in a senior university education course. *Journal of Educational Sociology, 35*(8), 346-354.

Blackburn, M. A., & Miller, R. B. (1996, April). *Cheating and motivation: A possible relationship.* Paper presented at the annual meeting of the American Educational Research Association, New York.

Bowers, W. J. (1964). *Student dishonesty and its control in college.* New York: Columbia University, Bureau of Applied Social Research.

Brandes, B. (1986). *Academic honesty: A special study of California students.* Sacramento, CA: California State Department of Education, Bureau of Publications.

Bruggeman, E. L., & Hart, K. J. (1996). Cheating, lying, and moral reasoning by religious and secular high school students. *Journal of Educational Research, 89*(6), 340-344.

Bunn, D. N., Caudill, S. B., & Gropper, D. M. (1992). Crime in the classroom: An economic analysis of undergraduate student cheating behavior. *Journal of Economic Education, 23*(3), 197-207.

Bushweller, K. (1999). Generation of cheaters. *American School Boards Journal, 186*(4), 24-32.

Calabrese, R. L., & Cochran, J. T. (1990). The relationship of alienation to cheating among a sample of American adolescents. *Journal of Research and Development in Education, 23*(2), 65-71.

California Education Code, §66400 (2001).

Cizek, G. J. (1999). *Cheating on tests: How to do it, detect it, and prevent it.* Mahwah, NJ: Lawrence Erlbaum.

Cizek, G. J. (2001). More unintended consequences of high-stakes testing. *Educational Measurement: Issues and Practice, 20*(4), 19-27.

Clouse, B. (1973). Attitudes of college students as a function of sex, politics, and religion. *Journal of College Student Personnel, 14*(3), 260-264.

Coady, H., & Sawyer, D. (1986). Moral judgment, sex, and level of temptation as determinants of resistance to temptation. *Journal of Psychology, 120*(2), 177-181.

Cole, N. (1998, November 9). Teen cheating hurts all. *USA Today,* p. 24A.

Cooper, S., & Peterson, D. (1980). Machiavellianism and spontaneous cheating in competition. *Journal of Research in Personality, 14*(1), 70-75.

Cornehlsen, V. H. (1965). Cheating attitudes and practices in a suburban high school. *Journal of the National Association of Women Deans and Counselors, 28*(1), 106-109.

Cumming, D. (1995, September 25). Competition, weak morals increasing cheating incidents. *Atlanta Journal and Constitution,* p. B-2.

Davis, B. G. (2002). *Preventing academic dishonesty.* Retrieved May 15, 2002, from http://teaching.berkeley.edu/bgd/prevent.html

Davis, S. F., Grover, C. A., Becker, A. H., & McGregor, L. N. (1992). Academic dishonesty: Prevalence, determinants, techniques, and punishments. *Teaching of Psychology, 19*(1), 16-20.

DePalma, A. (1992, May 2). The chase after cheaters on college-entry exams. *New York Times,* p. A1.

Dickstein, L. S., Montoya, R., & Neitlich, A. (1977). Cheating and fear of negative evaluation. *Bulletin of the Psychonomic Society, 10*(4), 319-320.

Diekhoff, G. M., LaBeff, E. E., Clark, R. E., Williams, L. E., Francis, B., & Haines, V. J. (1996). College cheating: Ten years later. *Research in Higher Education, 37*(4), 487-502.

Doster, J. T., & Chance, J. (1976). Interpersonal trust and trustworthiness in preadolescents. *Journal of Psychology, 93*(1), 71-79.

Drake, C. A. (1941). Why students cheat. *Journal of Higher Education, 12,* 418-420.

Eble, K. E. (1988). *The craft of teaching: A guide to mastering the professor's art.* San Francisco: Jossey-Bass.

Erickson, M. L., & Smith, W. B. (1974). On the relationship between self-reported and actual deviance: An empirical test. *Humboldt Journal of Social Relations, 1*(2), 106-113.

Evans, E. D., & Craig, D. (1990). Adolescent cognitions for academic cheating as a function of grade level and achievement status. *Journal of Adolescent Research, 5*(3), 325-345.

Feldman, S. E., & Feldman, M. T. (1967). Transition of sex differences in cheating. *Psychological Reports, 20*(3), 957-958.

Florida Statutes, Title XVI, S232.246, 5, c (2001).

Footer, N. S. (1996). Achieving fundamental fairness: The code of conduct. In W. L. Merced (Ed.), *Critical issues in judicial affairs: Current trends and practice* (pp. 19-33). San Francisco: Jossey-Bass.

Genereux, R. L., & McLeod, B. A. (1995). Circumstances surrounding cheating: A questionnaire study of college students. *Research in Higher Education, 36*(6), 687-704.

Graham, M. A., Monday, J., O'Brien, K., & Steffen, S. (1994). Cheating at small colleges: An examination of student and faculty attitudes and behaviors. *Journal of College Student Development, 35*(4), 255-260.

Gross, M. M. (1946). The effect of certain types of motivation on the honesty of children. *Journal of Educational Research, 40,* 133-140.

Guskey, T. R., & Bailey, J. M. (2001). *Developing grading and reporting systems for student learning.* Thousand Oaks, CA: Corwin Press.

Haines, V. J., Diekhoff, G. M., LaBeff, E. E., & Clark, R. E. (1986). College cheating: Immaturity, lack of commitment, and the neutralizing attitude. *Research in Higher Education, 25*(4), 342-354.

Haladyna, T. M. (1999). *A complete guide to student grading.* Boston: Allyn and Bacon.

Harp, L. (1995, May 3). Academic tourney's black mark: A cheating scandal. *Education Week,* pp. 1, 14.

Hartshorne, H., & May, M. A. (1928). *Studies in the nature of character: Vol. 1. Studies in deceit.* New York: Macmillan.

Hein, D. (1982). Rethinking honor. *Journal of Thought, 17*(1), 3-6.

Heisler, G. (1974). Ways to deter law violators: Effects of levels of threat and vicarious punishment on cheating. *Journal of Consulting and Clinical Psychology, 42*(4), 577-582.

Hetherington, E. M., & Feldman, S. E. (1964). College cheating as a function of subject and situational variables. *Journal of Educational Psychology, 55,* 212-218.

Hill, J. P., & Kochendorfer, R. A. (1969). Knowledge of peer success and risk of detection as determinants of cheating. *Developmental Psychology, 1*(3), 231-238.

Hoff, A. G. (1940). A study of the honesty and accuracy found in pupil checking of examination papers. *Journal of Educational Research, 34*(2), 127-129.

Houser, B. B. (1982). Student cheating and attitude: A function of classroom control technique. *Contemporary Educational Psychology, 7*(2), 113-123.

Houston, J. P. (1976). Learning and cheating as a function of study phase distraction. *Journal of Educational Research, 69*(7), 247-249.

Huss, M. T., Curnyn, J. P., Roberts, S. L., Davis, S. F., Yandell, L., & Giordano, P. (1993). Hard driven but not dishonest: Cheating and the type A personality. *Bulletin of the Psychonomic Society, 31*(5), 429-430.

Jacobellis v. Ohio. 378 U.S. 184 (1964).

Josephson, M. (1998). *Cheating leads to cheating.* Available at http://www.charactercounts.org/knxwk67.htm

Kahle, L. R. (1980). Stimulus condition self-selection by males in the interaction of locus of control and skill-chance situations. *Journal of Personality and Social Psychology, 38*(1), 50-56.

Keehn, J. D. (1956). Unrealistic reporting as a function of extraverted neuroses. *Journal of Clinical Psychology, 12,* 61-63.

Knowlton, J. Q., & Hamerlynck, L. A. (1967). Perception of deviant behavior: A study of cheating. *Journal of Educational Psychology, 58*(6), 379-385.

Kolich, A. M. (1983). Plagiarism: The worm of reason. *College English, 45*(2), 141-148.

Krebs, R. L. (1969). Teacher perceptions of children's moral behavior. *Psychology in the Schools, 6*(4), 394-395.

Lathrop, A., & Foss, K. (2000). *Student cheating and plagiarism in the Internet era.* Englewood, CO: Libraries Unlimited.

Leming, J. S. (1978). Cheating behavior, situational influence, and moral development. *Journal of Educational Research, 71*(4), 214-217.

Leveque, K. L., & Walker, R. E. (1970). Correlates of high school cheating behavior. *Psychology in the Schools, 7*(2), 159-163.

Levine, D. (1995, October). Cheating in our schools: A national scandal. *Reader's Digest,* 65-70.

Lipson, A., & McGavern, N. (1993, May). *Undergraduate academic dishonesty at MIT: Results of a study of attitudes and behavior of undergraduates, faculty, and graduate teaching assistants.* Paper presented at the 33rd annual forum for the Association for Institutional Research, Chicago. (ERIC Document Reproduction Service No. ED 368 272)

Lobel, T. E., & Levanon, I. (1988). Self-esteem, need of approval, and cheating behavior in children. *Journal of Educational Psychology, 80,* 122-123.

Ludeman, W. W. (1938). A study of cheating in public schools. *American School Board Journal, 96*(3), 45-46.

Mallon, T. (1989). *Stolen words.* New York: Ticknor and Fields.

McCabe, D. (2001). Cheating: Why students do it and how we can help them stop. *American Educator, 25*(4), 38-43.

McCabe, D. L. (1999). Academic dishonesty among high school students. *Adolescence, 34*(136), 681-687.

McCabe, D. L., & Bowers, W. J. (1996). The relationship between student cheating and college fraternity or sorority membership. *NASPA Journal, 33*(4), 280-291.

McCabe, D. L., & Trevino, L. K. (1993). Academic dishonesty: Honor codes and other contextual influences. *Journal of Higher Education, 64*(5), 522-538.

McGregor, J. H., & Streitenberger, D. C. (1998). Do scribes learn? Copying and information use. *SLMQ On-line.* [www.ala.org/aasl/SLMQ/scribes.html]

McLaughlin, R. D., & Ross, S. M. (1989). Student cheating in high school: A case of moral reasoning vs. "fuzzy" logic. *High School Journal, 72*(3), 97-104.

Mehrens, W. A., & Cizek, G. J. (2001). Standard setting and the public good: Benefits accrued and anticipated. In G. J. Cizek (Ed.), *Setting performance standards: Concepts, methods, and perspectives* (chap. 19, pp. 477-485). Mahwah, NJ: Lawrence Erlbaum.

Mehrens, W. A., & Lehmann, I. J. (1991). *Measurement and evaluation in education and psychology* (4th ed.). Fort Worth, TX: Holt, Rinehart and Winston.

Mixon, F. G., & Mixon, D. C. (1996). The economics of illegitimate activities: Further evidence. *Journal of Socioeconomics, 25*(3), 373-381.

Nowell, C., & Laufer, D. (1997). Undergraduate cheating in the fields of business and economics. *Journal of Economic Education, 28*(1), 3-12.

Ohio Revised Code, §3301-7-01, C1-C7 (1995).

O'Leary, M. (1999). The Web banishes term-paper blues. *Information Today, 16*(3), 14.

On plagiarism. (2002). Retrieved April 24, 2002, from http://www.2learn.ca/mapset/SafetyNet/plagiarism/plagiarismframes.html

Owasso Independent School District No. I-011 v. Falvo (No. 001073). U.S. Supreme Court, February 19, 2002.

Pearson, G. (2002). *Electronic plagiarism seminar.* Retrieved October 15, 2002, from http://www.lemoyne.edu/library/plagiarism.htm

Pennsylvania Code, Title 22, §4.24, a (1999).

Poppen, J. (2002, March 2). Mother of "boy genius" lied. *Rocky Mountain News*, p. B-1.

Revised Code of Washington, §28B, 10.580 (2002).

Roberts, J. M. (1976). *History of the world.* New York: Knopf.

Roig, M. (1997). Can undergraduate students determine whether text has been plagiarized? *Psychological Record, 47*(1), 113-122.

Roig, M., & DeTommaso, L. (1995). Are college cheating and plagiarism related to academic procrastination? *Psychological Reports, 77*(2), 691-698.

Roig, M., & Neaman, M. W. (1994). Alienation, learning or grade orientation, and achievement as correlates of attitudes toward cheating. *Perceptual and Motor Skills, 78*, 1096-1098.

Rost, D. H., & Wild, K. P. (1994). Cheating and achievement-avoidance at school: Components and assessment. *British Journal of Educational Psychology, 64*(1), 119-132.

Schab, F. (1969). Cheating in high school: Differences between the sexes. *Journal of the National Association of Women Deans and Counselors, 33*(1), 39-42.

Schab, F. (1991). Schooling without learning: Thirty years of cheating in high school. *Adolescence, 26*(104), 839-847.

Scheers, N. J., & Dayton, C. M. (1987). Improved estimation of academic cheating behavior using the randomized response technique. *Research in Higher Education, 26*(1), 61-69.

Schneider, A. (1999, January 22). Why professors don't do more to stop students who cheat. *Chronicle of Higher Education*, p. A-8.

Shelton, J., & Hill, J. P. (1969). Effects on cheating of achievement anxiety and knowledge of peer performance. *Developmental Psychology, 1*(5), 449-445.

Sierles, F. S., Hendrickx, I., & Circle, S. (1980). Cheating in medical school. *Journal of Medical Education, 55,* 124-125.

Sierles, F. S., Kushner, B. D., & Krause, P. B. (1988). A controlled experiment with a medical student honor system. *Journal of Medical Education, 63*(9), 705-713.

Singh, U. P., & Akhtar, S. N. (1972). Personality variables and cheating in examinations. *Indian Journal of Social Work, 32*(4), 423-428.

Standler, R. B. (2000). *Plagiarism in colleges in USA* [sic]. Available online at http://www.rbs2.com/plag.htm [retrieved May 31, 2002].

Steininger, M., Johnson, R., & Kirts, D. (1964). Cheating on college examinations as a function of situationally aroused anxiety and hostility. *Journal of Educational Psychology, 55*(6), 317-324.

Stevens, G. E., & Stevens, F. W. (1987). Ethical inclinations of tomorrow's managers revisited: How and why students cheat. *Journal of Education for Business, 61*(1), 24-29.

Sutton, E. M., & Huba, M. E. (1995). Undergraduate student perceptions of academic dishonesty as a function of ethnicity and religious participation. *NASPA Journal, 33*(1), 19-34.

Teacher resigns after classroom battle. (2002, January 25). Retrieved February 1, 2002, from www.kctv5.com/Global/stroy.asp?s=636651

Texas Penal Code, §32.50 (1997).

University of North Carolina at Chapel Hill. (2000). *The graduate school handbook, 2000-2001.* Chapel Hill, NC: Author.

Vitro, F. T., & Schoer, L. A. (1972). The effects of probability of test success, test importance, and risk of detection on the incidence of cheating. *Journal of School Psychology, 10*(3), 269-277.

Whitley, B. E., Jr. (1998). Factors associated with cheating among college students. *Research in Higher Education, 39,* 235-274.

Who's Who Among American High School Students. (1996). *Twenty-sixth annual survey of high achievers.* Lake Forest, IL: Author.

Who's Who Among American High School Students. (1998). *Twenty-ninth annual survey of high achievers.* Lake Forest, IL: Author.

Wisconsin Statutes and Annotations, Chap. 118.33, a, 1-2 (1999-2000).

Zastrow, C. H. (1970). Cheating among college graduate students. *Journal of Educational Research, 64,* 157-160.

Zelizer, G. L. (2002, March 27). Sermon sharing: Timesaver or sin? *USA Today,* p. 13A.

Author Index

Subject Index

**CORWIN
PRESS**

The Corwin Press logo—a raven striding across an open book—
represents the happy union of courage and learning. We are a
professional-level publisher of books and journals for K-12 educators,
and we are committed to creating and providing resources that
embody these qualities. Corwin's motto is "Success for All Learners."